Chocolat Chocolat

Chocolat Chocolat Cho
Chocolat Chocolat Cho
Chocolat Chocolat Cho
Chocolat Chocolat Cho
Chocolat Chocolat Cho
Chocolat Chocolat Cho
Chocolat Chocolat Cho
Chocolat Chocolat Cho
Chocolat Chocolat Cho
Chocolat Chocolat Cho
Chocolat Chocolat Cho
Chocolat Chocolat Cho
Chocolat Chocolat Cho
Chocolat Chocolat Cho
Chocolat Chocolat Cho
Chocolat Chocolat
Chocolat Chocolat
Chocolat Chocolat

Chocolat

First published in France in 2007 under the title
Les Arômes du chocolat, by Hachette Livre (Hachette Pratique)
Copyright © 2007 Hachette Livre (Hachette Pratique)

© Text Stéphan Lagorce
Photography by Éric Fénot
Styling by Delphine Brunet

An Hachette Livre UK Company
www.hachettelivre.co.uk

First published in Great Britain in 2008 by
Hamlyn, a division of Octopus Publishing Group Ltd
2–4 Heron Quays, London E14 4JP

Copyright © English edition
Octopus Publishing Group Ltd 2008

Original French edition
HACHETTE LIVRE (Hachette Pratique) 2007

Distributed in the United States and Canada by
Hachette Book Group USA,
237 Park Avenue, New York, NY 10017 USA

ISBN 978 0 600 61904 8

Printed and bound in China

1 3 5 7 9 10 8 6 4 2

*This book contains dishes that are made with raw or lightly cooked eggs.
These should be avoided by vulnerable people such as pregnant and nursing
mothers, invalids, the elderly, babies and young children.*

Chocolat

Stéphan Lagorce

Photography
Éric Fénot

Styling
Delphine Brunet

OCTOPUS PUBLISHING GROUP

CONTENTS

INTRODUCTION

Is another book about chocolate really necessary?
It's a subject on which much has already been written, a lot of advice
given, and many recipes—good or otherwise—offered to the reader.
The editor, the author, the designer, and most of the professionals who
came together to make this book asked themselves this very question.

The subject of tasting chocolate quickly became an obvious angle,
since there is very little about it in cookery writing.
This book therefore focuses on the idea of discovering and
savoring quality chocolate. How should chocolate be sampled?
Using what criteria? What goes with it? How and when?
These are just some of the questions that this book seeks
to answer, offering ideas and suggestions to give a better
understanding and, finally, a better appreciation of chocolate,
this marvelous, complex product.

First, we present the different forms in which chocolate comes
(bars, powder, spread), and then offer the reader the keys to a
successful tasting. How can each of the five senses be stimulated to
an effective appreciation of chocolate's myriad flavors?
This involves classic combinations (chocolate and cigars, chocolate
and coffees) or more unusual ones (chocolate and flowers,
chocolate and spices) that can enhance chocolate.

Next come 40 essential recipes, the "fundamentals" of cooking with
chocolate, from which all variants, fantasies, and even follies derive.
Finally, a book on chocolate would not be complete without practical
advice on how to buy and store it or how it is made, plus tips and tricks
for using it in cooking. We even give some information on chocolate
around the world and the festivals with which it is associated.

Chocolate is a universal product. We aim to shed light on lesser-known
aspects and to celebrate its inexhaustible riches. Lavishly illustrated,
concise, strictly practical and accessible, this book will enchant all lovers
of chocolate, from connoisseurs to chocoholics.

Good tasting!

A CHOCOLATE
TASTING

TYPES OF CHOCOLATE: BARS

Chocolate-lovers are spoiled: supermarkets and specialist chocolate shops carry a lavish range of different bars of chocolate. Here are some guidance notes to the types that are on sale and the extraordinary variety available.

Dark chocolate

Dark or plain chocolate is made from cocoa (not less than 35%) in the form of a paste, powder, or butter. Sugar is also added, as is an emulsifier and sometimes a flavor. The trend is for a higher percentage of cocoa: some products contain 55%, 70%, 85%, or even 99% cocoa. The more cocoa the product contains, the less sugar, therefore the higher the percentage of cocoa, the stronger and more bitter the chocolate.

White chocolate

This is made from cocoa butter (20% minimum), powdered milk, an emulsifier, and often some kind of flavoring. It is light in color and does not contain cocoa solids or powder.

Milk chocolate

This is an intermediate formula between dark and white chocolate, containing cocoa (25% minimum), sugar, whole milk powder, lacto-serums, an emulsifying agent and, very often, some flavoring. Some "rich milk" or "full-cream" products may have been enriched with cream.

Dessert chocolate

Three kinds of chocolate (dark, white, and milk) are sold as "dessert" chocolates. They contain the same ingredients but are developed and formulated to melt easily with no lumps.

"Specialty" chocolate

This fashionable category encompasses chocolates from all four of the preceding categories, to which a variety of ingredients have been added, such as nuts, praline (ground caramelized almonds or hazelnuts), orange peel, coconut, cocoa, or mint flavoring, or even peppery spices.

Grands crus: single origin or single estate chocolates

These chocolates come from a single region or plantation and have a particular taste specific to their place of production, like *appellation contrôlée* wines or single malt whiskies. Here characteristic flavors are looked for and to bring them out the products have a high cocoa content, often 70% or even more.

Fairtrade and organic chocolates

These contain the same ingredients as others of their kind and are also subject to the same commercial regulations as other chocolates. They should contain at least 95% organic ingredients and are generally delicious.

TYPES OF CHOCOLATE: OTHER PRODUCTS

As well as chocolate bars, there are more treats—and ways for real chocoholics to enjoy chocolate at any hour of day or night.

Cocoa powder

This is the very "soul" of chocolate, the source of its flavor and its color. Cocoa powder is made when cacao paste is pressed to remove its cocoa butter; the remaining cocoa solids are processed to make fine unsweetened cocoa powder. Another process, alkalinization, enhances the color. Bitter, strong, and heady, cocoa is the basis for many drinks, recipes, and desserts.

Chocolate powder

This is made from cocoa powder (at least 32%), sugar, and, usually, an emulsifying agent, reinforced by flavoring. Note that it can be "lowfat" or "light," depending on its cocoa butter content.

Instant powders and drinks

Loved by children and manufactured by big companies, these contain the same ingredients as chocolate powders, with the addition of powdered milk, cereals, or nuts, and sometimes vitamins.

Chocolate spread

Here a well-known brand dominates the market, although other products exist. Commercial spreads are industrial variants of the traditional ganache (chocolate cream). They often contain little cocoa (less than 10%) but plenty of sugar, vegetable oil, and nuts. An emulsifier keeps the product from separating.

Filled and coated chocolate confectionery

Specialist chocolate-makers maintain this tradition and commercial brands rival them in inventing new varieties, especially around Christmas and other holiday times. Most of these varied products have a chocolate coating or shell (dark, white, or milk chocolate) combined with a filling (praline, ganache, fruits, peel, or gianduja, a nut paste).

Eggs and shapes

These are made by molding dark, milk, or white chocolate. The two half-eggs are shaped, chilled, turned out of the mold, and assembled by sticking together with melted chocolate.

Liqueur chocolates

These are chocolate shells containing either liqueurs distilled to a strength up to 77°F developed by steeping roasted beans, or very sugary, syrupy "creams," sometimes including real cream, infused with a liqueur. They are usually served with dessert or to flavor various puddings.

HOW TO TASTE

First and foremost, a chocolate tasting should combine a great deal of pleasure with a touch of technique. For the enlightened amateur who wishes to appreciate all chocolate's subtleties, a few guidelines about what is called "taste" may be useful. Here are some to bear in mind:

"Taste" or "tastes"?

When tasting chocolate, of whatever kind or quality, the "taste" that is registered is in fact the culmination of three sensations: gustatory, olfactory, and physical.

Gustatory sensations

These are revealed by the taste buds, little protrusions that cover the tongue. Put simply, they register the bitterness, acidity, and sugary content of a chocolate.

Olfactory sensations

These are delivered by nerve-endings in the nose; food is never in direct contact with them. They are extremely sensitive and can register the full aromatic palette of a great cacao: roasted, spicy, or smooth notes, for example.

Physical sensations

These are signaled by the whole mouth and convey the sample's hot, cold, piquant, or astringent character along with information about its texture, melting quality, graininess, or smoothness. Their true scientific name is "somatosensory perceptions."

A practical test

1

Pop a square of dark chocolate in your mouth; take 20 seconds to analyze its taste, then try to identify the gustatory, olfactory, and physical sensations it delivers.

2

Carry out the same test while pinching your nostrils shut—then compare the results!

I taste or I like?

We tend to judge everything we eat in terms of "I like" or "I don't like."

This is a conditioned reflex that needs to be adjusted when learning how to "taste" something. A degree of objectivity is required when assessing a chocolate. This is a question of knowing how to analyze your perceptions (sweet, strong, sugary) rather than judging by personal, rather "egocentric" preferences.

For example: I do not like sugar, therefore I may find a good-quality white chocolate "poor" and a poor-quality dark chocolate "good," simply because the latter is less sugary. In a first tasting you should aim to get an impression of the chocolate and to describe its particular points then, only at a second attempt, try to evaluate it.

A practical test

1

Taste a chocolate that you really like.

2

List its qualities in five words.

3

Be aware that your judgments will always be influenced by these values, which are personal to you. Rein them in!

TASTING WITH THE FIVE SENSES

Taste is not the only guideline to sampling chocolate. That would be like looking at a landscape with only one eye, since chocolate confectionery, bars, and ganaches involve all of the five senses. Here are some explanations.

Sight

This is the first sense with which we make contact with chocolate. It is therefore essential and should not be neglected. Begin by evaluating the color of the product: is it dark brown, black, white, in between? The darker it is, the richer in cocoa. Then assess the density of the colors: maybe one chocolate is dark brown and another a bit lighter? The cocoa beans may have been roasted more in one sample than in another. Next observe the gloss, which signals that the cocoa mass has been well tempered, molded, and cooled. Is the chocolate dull? The cocoa butter may have crystallized badly while cooling. Be careful!

Smell

The aroma of a chocolate conveys something about its life. Is the smell strong or weak? This is a good indicator of the percentage of cocoa and the quality of the roast. Is it sweet, musky, spicy, or neutral? Single origin chocolates have a pronounced smokiness that lesser quality chocolate does not have. Can you detect a slightly unpleasant note? In such cases, the chocolate may have aged badly or has dried out.

Taste

As far as this is concerned, it's important to concentrate on the degree of sweetness. Is it balanced or too strong? Is there an acid taste? Is it perceptible? If yes, to what degree? Too much acidity may indicate badly fermented or badly dried cocoa beans. Finally, is there a slight or pronounced bitterness? These are all indicators of the percentage of cocoa and the degree of roasting.

Touch

Chocolate is also sampled with the fingers! Is the surface smooth or slightly rough? Does it begin to melt as soon as you touch it, or not? Does it seem smooth or silky? The answers to these various questions will enable you to judge the cocoa butter content of a chocolate and the fineness of the micrograins of cacao it contains.

Hearing

Hearing also has a part to play in a chocolate tasting. When you break a block or squares do you hear a dry, brief "snap" or does the chocolate yield gradually and silently? In the first case, the chocolate is definitely too cold to be sampled under optimum conditions, in the second, it is probably too warm.

A practical exercise

1

Take two bars: one of dark chocolate containing 70% cocoa and one of white chocolate. Smell and touch them, noting their differences, then break them.

2

Repeat the exercise with two chocolates that are less dissimilar and note their differences.

THE EQUIPMENT NEEDED FOR A CHOCOLATE TASTING

It's easy to organize a little chocolate tasting with friends since the necessary implements are readily available. They will make all the difference, however, and will help toward a better perception of all the subtlety of the chocolates, whether they come as bars, confectionery, drinking chocolate, or chocolate liqueurs.

For tasting bars of chocolate

Depending on the varieties of chocolates that you want to sample, use white or clear glass plates or saucers. In each case, the chocolates should not touch each other and should be spaced at least ½ inch apart. Some manufacturers sell chocolate tasting samples in small squares or rounds. Use a pair of small tongs to lift the chocolate for observation and sampling. Avoid touching with the fingers.

For tasting chocolate spreads

Chocolate spreads should be sampled with small spoons such as coffee spoons. These hold three times less than an ordinary teaspoon, so you can taste the same product several times without overdoing it. Help yourself to the spread with these small spoons, then leave them on white plates. Do not taste more than four different products in a single session; they are high in fat and will soon saturate the palate.

For tasting drinking chocolate

To sample drinking chocolates properly, always choose clear or white cups. You will be better able to appreciate all the tints, colors, and nuances. Dark brown cocoa looks unattractive if served in a green, yellow, or red cup. You can use cups, bowls, or glasses but always go for fine-rimmed ones. A 5–7 fl oz serving is ample. Also provide small spoons to stir or add sugar to the chocolate.

For tasting liqueur chocolate

Present them in brandy glasses or large, thin glasses that will release the aromas so they become easily detectable. Serve the liqueur and leave in the glass for around 5 minutes before sampling.

HOW TO TASTE CHOCOLATE IN BARS

How do you assess bars of chocolate, which range from rich, sugary, white chocolate to powerful, bitter, dark chocolate with an 80% cocoa content? What are the best methods? How should a tasting be organized? It's fun to gather a few friends to sample several different chocolates and to compare views. You may find that a single product will get many different opinions.

Why hold a tasting?

For pleasure and for a better understanding of this wonderful product. It's not necessary to make the complex technical "sensory analysis" that manufacturers use to taste and describe their products in scientific terms. If you learn enough to know how to appreciate chocolates, identify differences and explain some of them, you will quickly become an enlightened connoisseur able, for instance, to distinguish different levels of cocoa.

How many people at a tasting?

There are really no rules; everything depends on how much space you have available. Six or eight people will make a group that can work well together. More than that, things may get a bit confused.

What products to use for a joint tasting?

It would not make sense to compare a white chocolate with a single origin cocoa. The differences are too great and the palate, faced with too great a difference, will lose its capacity to judge. The golden rule for a successful and coherent tasting is to assess comparable chocolate "families" (see "Types of Chocolate," pages 11 and 12). You could also have specialty tastings: "dark chocolates," "milk chocolates," "drinking chocolates," and so on.

How many products should be tasted in one session?

Here it is difficult to lay down strict rules; we can only advise. Chocolate is a rich, sensuous, aromatic, fatty product that quickly creates a feeling of "saturation." The palate is very susceptible to rich flavors and, depending on the individual, will quickly lose its edge. Here are advisable quantities for a successful tasting.

Dark and single origin chocolates
No more than 8–10 different products.

Milk chocolate
No more than 6–8 different products.

White chocolate
No more than 4–6 products.

Specialties
No more than 4–6 products.

Tasting order and time

Always start by tasting the "weakest" chocolates, moving gradually through the strengths to the most powerful. For dark chocolates, in particular, begin with those with a 35% minimum cocoa content then move on to higher percentages, not the opposite. Allow at least 1–2 minutes for each type of chocolate. Write down your impressions as you go along, then make further notes on how each product compares with others.

Dos and don'ts
· Do not prepare tasting plates more than 30 minutes in advance and do not touch the chocolate with your fingers: break bars through the foil wrapper.
· Do not provide more than 2 squares of the same chocolate per person.
· The best times for tasting are from 11 am–12.30 pm and 7–9 pm.
· Avoid tasting after a heavy meal.
· Take a drink of water at room temperature between two different chocolates.

HOW TO TASTE
DRINKING CHOCOLATES

For a tasting, several types of drinking chocolate should be served at the same temperature and time, to make it easier to compare them.

Making drinking chocolate

Unsweetened cocoa powders are all prepared in the same way.
Allow 1 teaspoon cocoa, 1 teaspoon sugar, and ½ cup measure of milk.
Heat this mixture to just below boiling point, let it cool for 5 minutes, then serve. However, always read the maker's instructions.

Preparing the serving dishes

Warm the tasting glasses, bowls, or cups in hot water or in a low oven (140°F), then dry well. Serve the drinks as soon as they are ready; that way your guests will be better able to judge the smoothness and creaminess of the products. Have small spoons available.

The order of tasting,
number of products, quantities, and temperature

Begin with the powerful, aromatic bitter cocoas and follow them with the instant mixtures. Do not sample more than four or five drinks in one tasting. A 5 fl oz cup of each chocolate is plenty.
The ideal serving temperature is 113–122°F.

The tasting

Taste the drinks one by one and immediately write down your observations on a sheet of paper (is the flavor rich, weak, complex, simple, bitter, too sugary …?) Having tasted all the products, compare them with each other and classify them, for example in order of strength, complexity, or other considerations. Then, and only then, put them in order of preference. Next, share your observations with everyone.

With milk or water? With sugar or without?
It's worth considering this point with bitter chocolate (100% cocoa).
Yes, it's delicious made with milk and with sugar added, but some of the drink's aromatic richness is masked. If you simply dilute with water you will discover the infinite variety of flavors that bitter chocolates can offer. At first, this may taste odd but the experience is unique and educational.

HOW TO TASTE CHOCOLATE-BASED DESSERTS

*You wouldn't sample a chocolate cake as you would a sabayon,
or a chocolate ice like a sweet. To appreciate all the subtleties of a dessert
made with cocoa or chocolate, here is some simple advice.*

Cakes

Ideally they should be sampled within two or three hours after cooking.
In a cake recipe, chocolate flavors mingle with those of butter, flour, and eggs.
Little by little they lose their strength. Don't delay!

Mousses and fondants

Fondants should be unmolded quickly but gently so that they don't break,
and eaten as soon as possible. Serve immediately while the center is
still liquid and before it continues to cook through thermal inertia.
Provide small spoons for a successful tasting.

Confectionery

Serve chilled, if possible around 46–53°F. Maybe you have a wine cellar?
Chocolate truffles and bouchées have an intense aroma and the palate
loses its sensitivity after a few minutes. Remember to drink a little water
between each sweet to clear the palate. If you have several types
of bouchées or truffles, always finish with those containing alcohol
or flavoring, whether of praline, spices, or tea.

Ices

Chocolate ice cream is at its most delicious when it comes out of
the ice-cream maker. If you leave it in the freezer, the ice crystals
will fuse together and the ice cream will turn into a solid lump,
disguising the flavors.

Hot sauces

They should never be served at a temperature higher than 132°F,
which is the point at which a "burning" sensation is felt. Don't pour the
sauce over desserts until the last minute or it will lose its gloss.

Macaroons

If plain, eat them soon after cooking. If you plan to decorate them,
wait a day (if you can!): the filling will gently relax the dough
and make it meltingly delicious.

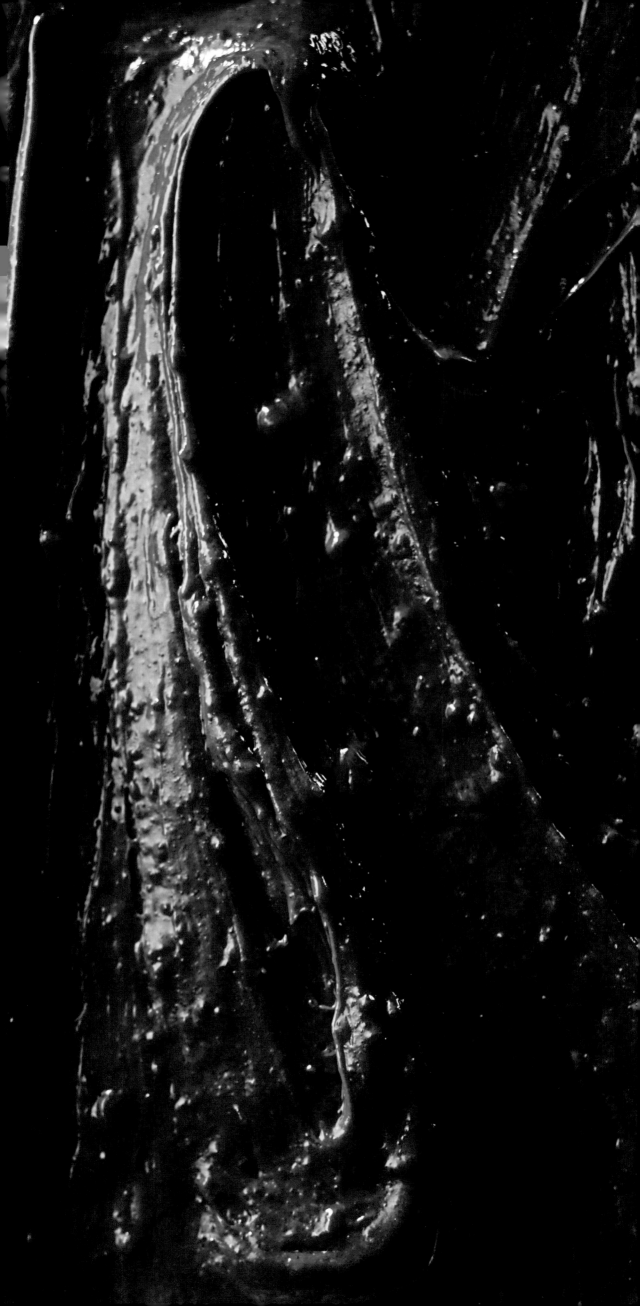

A tasting glossary

Here are some terms used in tasting chocolate,
along with their meaning.

❧❧

Texture

Crisp
This applies if the chocolate snaps with a clean break.
The "snap" of a dark chocolate is quite different to that of a milk chocolate.

✳

Melting
This defines the rapidity with which a chocolate melts in the mouth
while being tasted.

✳

Grainy/floury
These terms are used to describe the size, shape, and quantity of particles
that can be detected.

✳

Greasy
Used to describe the fattiness or otherwise of the taste in the mouth.

✳

Thick/sticky
Said of a chocolate that seems difficult to melt in the mouth.

✳

Dry
Describes a chocolate that takes a long time to melt in the mouth.

❧❧

Taste

Acid
Some highly fermented beans can make rather acidic chocolate.

✳

Aggressive
This corresponds to the speed with which the taste becomes
apparent in the mouth.

✳

Bitter
Bitterness is typical of dark chocolates that have a high cocoa content.

✳

Cacao-y
This means the amount of cacao present and is most often
applied to dark chocolates.

✳

Intense
This applies to the sustained taste of the chocolate.

✳

Milky
Used if a taste or smell of milk, cream, or butter is present;
obviously relates only to milk and white chocolate.

Medium
This term defines a chocolate of average underlying taste.

✳

Subtle
Used to describe a chocolate of less pronounced taste.

✳

Sugary
Not all chocolates have the same degree of sugariness.

≈≈

Flavor

Animal
Some chocolates, generally dark ones, develop deep musky notes,
known as "animal."

✳

Spicy
During roasting, cocoa beans release many aromas.
Depending on origin and the process used, some of them are spicy.

✳

Floral
Some grands crus produce cacaos with light notes, often described
as "floral" or "flowery."

✳

Grilled
This term characterizes the intensity of the chocolate's roasted notes.

✳

Vanilla
Vanilla flavors are typical of many white and milk chocolates.

Useful tips
When tasting a chocolate, try to differentiate between the "attacking" aromatic notes,
which can be identified within 4–5 seconds of tasting, and the "base" notes,
which take longer to develop but are very powerful.

Technical glossary

Alkalinization
A process used to darken the color of cocoa powders.

✻

Bean
The term used for both the fruit of the cacao tree and the contents of the cacao bean, from which the cacao is made.

✻

Cacao
The substance produced from the cacao bean. Cacao paste is the prime ingredient of all cacao-based products. It is obtained by grinding beans that have first been cleaned, husked, and roasted. Cacao contains between 45–55% of fatty matter. Cocoa butter is extracted from this paste, which then solidifies and hardens. It keeps well in this state. Alternatively, the "cake" left in the grinder can be chopped and crushed, yielding a cocoa powder whose fat content is determined by the degree of pressure used when extracting the butter.

✻

Chocolate confectionery
These have various chocolate-coated fillings and are usually called just chocolates. They can be flavored with praline, gianduja, alcohol, spices, aromatics, or tea.

✻

Cocoa butter
The fatty matter obtained by grinding cacao. It gives texture, shape, and melting quality to the chocolate.

✻

Conching
This operation blends the chocolate mixture at a precise temperature to smooth the texture of the cocoa butter. This vital process determines the final smoothness and quality of the chocolate.

✻

Couverture
Also called dipping or coating chocolate, this is dark, milk, or white chocolate, sold in large blocks for professional use.

✻

Enrobing
The process by which confectionery is given a chocolate coating. The confectionery moves along a conveyor belt under a "shower" of chocolate. It can also be hand-dipped using a special fork.

✻

Ganache
Ganache or chocolate cream is made by mixing chocolate with cream, crème fraîche, or butter. It can be left plain or flavored.

✻

Gianduja
A paste made with roasted nuts, sugar, and melted chocolate.

✻

Nibs

Small fragments of cocoa bean kernels, fermented and dried, sometimes roasted.

✳

Nougatine

A light caramel mixed with roasted, chopped almonds, sometimes with hazelnuts added. Nougatine can be shaped or rolled into a slab.

✳

Praline

A mixture of blanched almonds or sometimes hazelnuts, lightly caramelized and then finely ground.

✳

Roasting

This process creates and enhances the flavor of the cocoa beans.

✳

Tempering

Bringing the chocolate to a given temperature to enhance its shine and texture.

GOOD THINGS TO GO WITH CHOCOLATE

CHOCOLATE AND WINE

Matching wines to foods is always an inexact science and laying down strict rules doesn't make sense: what may seem delicious to one person may not appeal to another. Beauty is more often in the eye of the beholder than in the pairing itself. So be careful. Here are a few suggestions to start you on the quest for these delicate balances.

Try a **Gewurztraminer vendanges tardives** with squares of classic, fairly bitter dark chocolate. Its aromas of candied fruit and spices are very elegant. You could also try a **Sauternes**, whose heady flowery bouquet may be deeper and more appealing.

You might like to try a less complex but equally interesting pairing by offering a **Banyuls grand cru** served at 54–63°F (not too chilled), with a "grand cru" or single origin chocolate from Tanzania or Venezuela.

Specialist chocolate suppliers and some supermarkets sell high quality milk chocolates that deserve better than to be hastily eaten as a snack. They go well with the crystallized fruit, spices, and honey aromas of an aged, ruby-red **Rivesaltes**.

For sweet, mouth-filling (good) white chocolates, try **white ports** or **liqueurs**.

Some red wines go well with chocolates. Always serve them in small glasses: their aromas should bring out those of the chocolate, not mask them. Try pairing a square of dark 70% chocolate with the fruit liqueur and vanilla aromas of a **Côte-rôtie**. Do the same with a **Pommard**: the tannins work well with the cocoa's roasted notes. Finally, not to overlook rosé wine, try a square of good milk chocolate with a quality **Tavel**; the fresh sensation will surprise you!

CHOCOLATE AND SPIRITS

*Strong liquors are easier than wines to match up with chocolates.
Their aromas and low acidity make them a "natural" complement to
chocolate's sugary and fatty taste. When tasting, spirits should
be served in small quantities; another technique is simply to dip
the chocolate squares in the alcohol.*

Armagnacs

Discover or rediscover the power of a dark chocolate sampled with
a delicate, fruity Bas Armagnac (low in alcohol and high in acidity).
If you enjoy long-lasting, sensuous flavors, pair an aged, amber-colored
Ténarèze Armagnac with a 90 or 99% dark chocolate. Sensational!

Cognacs

Serve a Grande or Petite Champagne Cognac in a brandy glass.
Allow it to "breathe" for a minute then try it with a premium gianduja from
Central America or one from the Caribbean, possibly even more classic.
The flavors of this pairing are so complex that your palate will
have difficulty telling them apart—but in a pleasurable way.

Single malt whiskies

Chocolates go very well with whiskies, which bring out their flavor.
If you appreciate light but rounded and supple single malts, match them
with truffles or ganache-filled confectionery. If you prefer the endless
complexity and smoothness of peaty whiskies, pair them with
praline- or gianduja-flavored chocolates.

Rum

Select an agricultural rum, made exclusively from fermented and
distilled cane sugar. The vanilla and freshly baked cake bouquet is
a splendid match for Caribbean grand cru chocolate and goes
equally well with milk and white chocolate.

Tequila

Tequila or "agave wine" is a spirit that works well with chocolate.
It highlights complex or roasted flavors or even the slight acidity
of single-varietal milk chocolates such as the criollos or
forasteros (see page 152).

Vodka

Save vodka for certain chocolate desserts such as ices, mousses,
and fondants (see pages 125, 59, and 90). Serve it iced in small glasses and
enjoy the contrast of its well-balanced smoothness and attack.

CHOCOLATE AND COFFEES

Coffee and chocolate are so close that they could be called cousins. They come from almost the same geographical zones and share some of the manufacturing processes, such as roasting.

It's not surprising, therefore, that they go so well together. The current fashion is for "single estate," "pure Colombian," pure "Nicaraguan," and so on, but the best coffees will always be the balanced blends of different harvests and origins.

Robusta and Arabica

Caffeine-heavy, rather bitter robustas probably go better with relatively sugary chocolates like 52% dark ones, milk chocolates, confectionery, and truffles. Arabicas are more acidic but very aromatic, especially those from Nicaragua or Kenya. Serve them with chocolate confectionery such as fudge, mendiants, or candied orange peel (see pages 67, 68, and 70). If you prefer more subtle flavors, blend or buy a robusta–arabica mix and make it quite strong for a perfect accompaniment to macaroons, dacquoises, or madeleines.

Mocha

For a more unusual taste experience, choose the succulent mocha from the high Ethiopian plateaux of Harar or Sidamo. This premium coffee is characterized by its very low caffeine content and its delicate, perfumed taste. It would be perfect with a dark 70% chocolate, eaten alone, or to accompany a chocolate tart, pound cake, or butter-chocolate squares (see pages 130, 97, and 99).

Blue Mountain

This even rarer coffee is cultivated on the slopes of Jamaica's Blue Mountain. A very refined arabica, it is delightfully fragrant, low in acidity, mild, and fine, with a uniquely delicate bouquet. It goes superbly with a single origin dark chocolate or with a delicate hot soufflé (see page 116).

CHOCOLATE AND FLOWERS: HOW TO PAIR THEM

Thanks to specialist chocolatiers and inventive confectioners, flowers have found their natural affinity with chocolate. There is some degree of experimentation in such pairings, or perhaps it's a kind of culinary or gourmet "alchemy" for there are some amazing marriages. Flowers and chocolate can be combined in several ways and in each case the flowers may be fresh, dried, or candied.

Infusions/decoctions

Infuse flower petals (as if making a tisane) in milk and/or cream to be used in a ganache (see page 57). Remove the petals before using the cream, leaving only their scent to perfume the chocolate. You can also use lavender, sweet violet, lime-flowers, rose petals, jasmine, or thyme leaves as a filling for confectionery or desserts.

Enfleurage

This is an ancient but simple technique that consists of leaving squares or pieces of chocolate in contact with flowers in a sealed container for several days or hours. Enfleurage is most effective if highly scented flowers or herbs are used (lavender, thyme, orange, chives, jasmine, violets, or fuchsias) with relatively neutral chocolates such as milk or white chocolate or low-cocoa dark chocolate.

Incorporation

Here, the flowers are chopped or ground, roughly or finely (depending on the case and the desired result), then added to melted chocolate, ganaches, mousses, ices, or even to fillings. It is best to choose flowers with fairly soft petals as they remain in the chocolate and will be eaten. Try rose, hollyhock, sunflower, carnation, and even tulip petals.

Dipping/enrobing

In this case the flower, or its petals, is simply dipped (fresh, blanched, or candied) in melted chocolate. Zucchini flowers dipped in a 70% dark chocolate make very original confections, and do try roses or sunflowers. Small dandelion flowers blanched and dipped in white chocolate taste amazing.

Useful tips
Not all flowers are edible; some can be toxic. If in any doubt, buy them from a herbalist or check with a pharmacist.

CHOCOLATE AND TEA

Teas can give chocolate wonderfully refined flavors. There are many possible combinations or "recipes." We prefer not to make strict rules, or to list "good" or "bad" combinations, but here are a few suggestions for you to try out.

Tea for a chocolate tasting

Green teas

Their slight bitterness and their floral notes go well with a good quality white chocolate, which is quite sweet and sugary.

Yellow teas

Quite rare but prized by connoisseurs, lightly infused yellow teas will bring out the toasted notes of a Caribbean single origin chocolate.

White teas

If not served too hot, these light and almost translucent teas will temper the strength of dark chocolates with a high cocoa content, 70% and over.

Red teas

Their woody, fermented bouquet and their smoothness go well with chocolate creams. They enhance milk chocolate surprisingly. To appreciate such combinations properly, serve the tea warm, without sugar.

Tea in chocolate recipes

Tarry souchong ganache

This tea's smoky aromas give an unusual flavor to neutral dark chocolates or those with a low cocoa content (52%). Follow the instructions on page 57 to make an aromatic ganache, infusing the cream with a scant half-teaspoonful of tarry souchong. Remember to remove it before blending in the grated chocolate. Use this ganache to make truffles (see page 127).

Lapsang souchong ganache

This less smoky but full-bodied tea is delicious. Make the ganache as on page 57, using milk and dark chocolate in equal quantities and infusing the cream with a few pinches of tea. Follow the recipe as indicated.

Some combinations

· Serve a lightly brewed (2–3 minutes) oolong tea with a few squares of 99% dark chocolate for a delightful contrast.
· Try matcha green tea with a good milk chocolate with almond or hazelnut filling.
· Serve jasmine tea with a chilled dark chocolate mousse; the contrast of the tea's floral notes and the mousse's rich sweetness is a unique sensation.

CHOCOLATE AND CIGARS

The best cigars are fine on their own, of course, as are the best chocolates, but it's very tempting to try them together. Their colors and nuances are so similar: a handsome dark, mellow Maduro-wrapped cigar calls to mind a great deep brown 70% Guanaja. Always combine cigars with dark chocolates and remember that a powerful cigar will overwhelm any dessert or patisserie.

Hoyo de Monterrey, the princely Hoyo

Entirely handmade, this cigar opens with vanilla notes, evolving slowly into heavier, peaty, sensuous aromas. Try a dark 99% cocoa chocolate with it; it's probably the only one able to stand up to this "prince" of cigars.

Romeo y Julieta Belicosos

This great Cuban cigar is probably lighter but more subtle than the Hoyo (opinions are divided). At first its flavor is reminiscent of gingerbread, then of coffee grounds. Try it with squares of a dark Caribbean chocolate of at least 70% cocoa content, having first refrigerated it for 30 minutes to make it crisper.

Montecristo No. 1

Heavenly mellowness, unquestionably—or its earthly incarnation! A cigar to be prepared and smoked very gently in case it catches fire. The bouquet of honey, cinnamon, cardamom, and juniper make each puff a real trip. Match it with a praline chocolate or a Central American single estate with notes of exotic wood and liquorice.

Useful tip
For best appreciation of these complex combinations, taste no more than a half- or even quarter-square of chocolate each time. Put the chocolate on the tongue, let it melt and then, and only then, taste the cigar.

CHOCOLATE AND SPICES

With spices, you can let your imagination run riot: almost all experiences are possible. Rather like with flowers (see page 38) spices can be used in different ways according to the desired result. They can be infused in milk or cream so that only the aroma remains, or they can be incorporated ground or chopped, finely or otherwise, in bouchées, ganaches, cakes, mousses, and fillings.

Nutmeg

Generally only used in savory dishes, nutmeg brings a long, mellow flavor to mousses. Add it very finely ground to melted chocolate, using 3 or 4 pinches per 3½ oz (100 g) of chocolate.

Cardamom

This spice is little used in European cooking but deserves to be discovered or rediscovered. It goes well with bouchées and ganaches, ground, infused in cream, then filtered out.

Cloves

Hot and powerful, a clove should be used sparingly as its flavor will quickly dominate the other ingredients. Very finely ground, it gives an unexpected, agreeable flavor to cakes, cookies, or pound cake.

Black pepper

This is the immature, dried fruit of the pepper tree. Used in very small amounts it will bring a strong, savory flavor to ganaches and ices.

Sichuan "pepper"

Its unique aromas are less hot than black pepper and it gives truffles and ices a full-bodied mouth-feel. Use sparingly: a very tiny pinch for 7 oz (200 g) of chocolate.

Chiles

It's best to use these dried and chopped, whatever their strength. Piment d'Espelette, which is fruity and not burning hot, gives real character to fillings, fudges, and mendiants (a cookie).

Saffron

Used powdered or in strands, in small quantities—the tiniest pinch to 4½ oz (120 g) of chocolate—it brings a unique flavor and interesting personality to a white chocolate mousse and all recipes using white chocolate.

Cinnamon

Use ground cinnamon, in a ratio of a pinch to 3½ oz (100 g) of chocolate, preferably dark or white.

Ginger

Use fresh peeled root ginger to infuse fillings and ganaches, or chop crystallized ginger into them. It is superb in cakes, brownies, cookies, mousses, and sauces.

CHOCOLATE, NUTS, AND SEEDS

Nuts such as almonds or hazelnuts are traditionally associated with chocolate, especially in praline and gianduja, the bases for many bouchée fillings, but other nuts can also be used.

Coconut

Dessicated coconut is often blended with white chocolate (about 30%) to make a delicious ready-to-eat specialty. Truffles can also be rolled in it.

Walnuts

Walnuts go perfectly with dark chocolate; they are an essential ingredient in brownies, to which they give a penetrating flavor. Very finely ground, they can also be added to hot chocolate.

Pistachios

These green and savory nuts can be used whole or roughly chopped to decorate mendiants (see page 68).

Pecans

These flavorful nuts can be substituted for the classic walnuts in brownies.

Macadamia nuts

Bring out the flavor of these little round nuts by caramelizing them in a pan with a pinch of sugar, then add to a chocolate ice (see page 125).

Sesame seeds

Lightly toasted in a pan or in the oven, sesame seeds will flavor and decorate cakes, bouchées, and ganaches. If finely ground, they are called "tahini" and can be used to enrich chocolate cakes.

Poppy seeds

Poppy seeds have little taste but are very decorative and can be sprinkled over truffles, cookies (see pages 127 and 74), and bouchées.

Raisins

Raisins are inexpensive and widely available; they give flavor to cakes, especially if they are first soaked in a little rum.

CHOCOLATE AND VEGETABLES

Some vegetables seem sweeter than others! In fact, from this viewpoint there is no comparison between a carrot and spinach.
You only have to taste them. However, chocolate goes quite well with some vegetables—be brave and try.

Pumpkin

Its tender, sweet flesh is delicious. Cooked and finely chopped,
it can be added to ganaches (not more than 5–10%).
Roast pumpkin in the oven, then dice it and dip lightly in a dark
70% chocolate for a real delicacy. Well worth trying.

Fennel

Its aniseed flavor works wonders in slightly bitter ganaches: just infuse
the fennel in the cream. To accentuate the flavor, use the little
green fronds on top of the bulb.

Sweet chestnut

Its tender fragrant flesh tastes a bit like pumpkin, although it is firmer
and perhaps more assertive, making it more difficult to pair up with
chocolates. Try coating peeled and skinned blanched chestnuts with dark
chocolate, or pan-fry them and serve with a chocolate sauce.

Sweet potato

"Season" sweet potato chips with a mixture of spices (cinnamon, aniseed,
nutmeg) and bitter cocoa.

Red bell pepper

Cook strips of red bell pepper in honey then coat them in a light
layer of 70% dark chocolate. The mix of flavors is first intriguing,
then inviting. A real discovery.

Avocado

Add a little pinch of bitter cocoa to a vinaigrette made with honey
and serve with avocado halves.

Tomato

If possible, select the very sweet yellow varieties.
They can be eaten raw, sliced, and sprinkled at the very last minute
with a touch of bitter cacao. Small yellow cherry tomatoes,
dried or preserved, can be coated with dark chocolate.

ESSENTIAL RECIPES

THE BEST EQUIPMENT FOR COOKING WITH CHOCOLATE

While the equipment used by professional chocolate-makers ("chocolatiers") is impressive, you need only a few items for cooking at home. Here is a short list of absolutely indispensable items; you can add to it as you go along.

Thermometer

Choose one that goes from 32–175°F, which is quite adequate for working with chocolate. Easiest to use are those with a metal probe and a digital display, which is simple to read.

Spatula

This little utensil has a handle and a flat plastic or rubber head; it is very useful for blending melted chocolate (or chocolate that is melting) or for scraping mixtures from bowls. Try to have 2 or 3 of different sizes.

Mixing bowl

Chose a metal one as it conducts heat well, necessary when melting chocolate, except if using a microwave. Again, equip yourself with several: small, medium, and large.

Whisks

Go for the simplest types.
A whisk is indispensable for almost all mixtures here.

Molds and baking pans

Whether metal, non-stick, or silicone, equip yourself with as many as possible. You will need at least one charlotte mold, a high-sided pan, baking pans for tarts and madeleines, plus several others of different shapes and sizes.

Electric beater

Essential. Go for the simplest model.

Ice-cream maker

The type that you put in the freezer overnight gives very good results, although the amount of ice cream that can be prepared in one batch is limited. Free-standing, electrically operated models with built-in freezers are perfect but more expensive.

Mixer

An invaluable piece of equipment for dessert and cake making and almost indispensable for making macaroons.

Chocolate icing
intense

⌒⌒

What can be more elegant or appetizing than a cake beautifully iced with chocolate? Contrary to appearances, the technique of icing is relatively simple. Care in maintaining certain temperatures during the operation is the key to success.

½ cup unsalted butter
8 oz (250 g) 52% dark chocolate, grated

Serves 6–8 · Preparation time: 20 minutes
Essential equipment: thermometer

1
Melt the butter in a pan. Remove from the heat and leave to cool for 10 minutes. Use a tablespoon to skim off the foam on top of the melted butter then set aside the butter "oil" or clarified butter, discarding the milky liquid in the bottom of the pan.

2
Meantime, melt the dark chocolate in a barely warm water bath (double boiler) or in a heatproof bowl set over a pan of barely simmering water.

3
Remove the bowl of melted chocolate from the pan and use a thermometer to check that the temperature of the chocolate, as well as that of the butter, does not exceed 86°F. Pour the butter into the melted chocolate and blend with a plastic spatula.

Useful tips
· The optimum temperature for icing is between 77–86°F.
· Do not pour the icing over a cake that has not fully cooled.
· Pour the icing over the cake then tilt it to one side and the other to cover the whole.
· Do not spread it with a spatula.
· Do not ice a cake in a room where the temperature exceeds 86°F.
· Once iced, place the cake in the refrigerator.

Chocolate ganache
intense

∞∞

*Indispensable in much of confectionery, ganache—a chocolate cream
filling for cakes, cookies, and other gourmet delights—is in many
ways the pinnacle of the chocolate-maker's art. The basic recipe
is very simple, only the chocolate and cream are essential.
Once mastered, this recipe can be varied infinitely.*

Basic recipe for ganache
2½ oz (70 g) 70% dark chocolate
1¼ oz (30 g) 52% dark chocolate
Scant ½ cup crème fraîche
Makes about 7 oz (Serves 4–6) · Preparation time: 15 minutes

1
Using a large knife, flake the chocolates into more or less regular small pieces.
You could also grate them coarsely with a vegetable grater, or use ready-made
chocolate buttons or drops.

2
Bring the crème fraîche to just boiling point in a pan, then remove from
the heat. Add the chocolate and blend away from the heat.

3
When fully blended and shiny, pour the mixture into a bowl.
Depending on the recipe, use it immediately or let it cool, then refrigerate.
Uses: filling for cakes and bouchées.
Variations: prepare the recipe with milk or white chocolate.

🌿

Butter ganache
7 oz (200 g) chocolate (dark, milk, white, or a mixture)
Scant ½ cup crème fraîche
3 tablespoons unsalted butter
Makes about 12 oz (Serves 4–6) · Preparation time: 15 minutes

Prepare this ganache as in the preceding recipe, adding the soft butter
to the crème fraîche at the same time as the chopped chocolate.
Uses: bouchées, confectionery. If poured into a bowl while still warm and left overnight
in the refrigerator, this ganache can be cut into different shapes.

🌿

Flavored ganaches
7 oz (200 g) chocolate (dark, milk, white, or a mixture)
Scant ½ cup crème fraîche
Makes about 10 oz (Serves 4–6) · Preparation time: 25 minutes

Make the basic recipe but flavor the crème fraîche by infusing it for 10 minutes
with coffee, spices, herbs, teas, infusions, or your choice of aromatics.
Uses: truffles, cookies, macaroons.

🌿

Souffléd ganaches
7 oz (200 g) chocolate (dark, milk, white, or a mixture)
Scant ½ cup crème fraîche
Makes about 10 oz (Serves 4–6) · Preparation time: 25 minutes

Make the basic recipe then, without letting it cool down, beat for 10 minutes
at high speed with an electric beater. The ganache will become light and fluffy.
Uses: cookies, macaroons, truffles.

Dark chocolate mousse
intense

ᘓᘗ

*There are many recipes for chocolate mousse. Here is one that has,
among other advantages, the merit of being easy to make. Rich in cocoa,
it is not too sweet and generally appeals more to adults than children.*

2 tablespoons unsalted butter
7½ oz (230 g) 52% dark chocolate, grated
2½ oz (70 g) 70% or higher chocolate,
a single origin Central American brand, if possible
Scant ½ cup heavy cream
5 egg whites
⅜ cup confectioners' sugar
2 egg yolks
2 tablespoons bitter cocoa
Serves 4–6 · Preparation time: 35 minutes · Chilling time: 4 hours
Essential equipment: electric beater

1
Melt the butter and both chocolates in a water bath or a heatproof bowl
placed over a pan of warm water. Mix well with a wooden spoon.
Take care not to overheat the chocolate; the water should be just warm.

2
Bring the cream to boiling point in a pan and add to the chocolate. Mix well. Beat
the egg whites into stiff peaks then gradually add the confectioners' sugar.

3
Add the egg yolks to the chocolate-cream mixture then gently fold in
the egg whites, taking care not to stir too much or the peaks will collapse.
Transfer to the serving dish.

4
Refrigerate for at least 4 hours. Sprinkle the mousse with
bitter cocoa before serving.

Chocolate custard cream
medium

ⱷⱷ

*This is a classic custard cream, to be eaten on its own, still warm,
or as a filling for choux pastry items such as éclairs.*

3 cups lowfat milk
5 tablespoons bitter cocoa
⅔ cup superfine sugar
6 egg yolks
Scant ½ cup all-purpose flour
3 tablespoons cornstarch
3 tablespoons unsalted butter + extra for chilling
Serves 6–8 · Preparation time: 20 minutes

1
Put the milk and cocoa in a bowl and beat well. Whisk the sugar and egg yolks
in another bowl, add the flour and cornstarch, and mix well.

2
Pour the cocoa-milk mixture over the egg mixture, mix well, and pour into
a pan. Bring to boiling point over a low heat, whisking constantly.
As soon as the custard cream comes to a boil, allow it to cook for 5–10 seconds
then remove the pan from the heat. Add the butter and stir in.

3
Pour the chocolate custard cream into a dish, wipe a knob of butter over
the surface to prevent it crusting, and leave to cool.

Useful tips
· To ensure that the custard cream stays thick, do not let it boil for long.
· For a sweeter, less bitter taste, replace the bitter cocoa with a 52% dark chocolate.

Chocolate buttercream
medium

∽∾

*Indispensable to a delicious Yule log, buttercream also works well
as a filling for sponge cakes and macaroons.*

5 egg yolks
⅔ cup superfine sugar
2 tablespoons water
¾ cup softened unsalted butter
2 oz (60 g) 52% dark chocolate, grated
Serves 6–8 · Preparation time: 20 minutes
Essential equipment: electric whisk, sugar thermometer

1
Using a medium bowl, beat the egg yolks at maximum speed for 7–8 minutes.
Meanwhile put the sugar and water in a pan and bring to
a boil until it becomes syrupy.

2
When the sugar-syrup reaches a temperature of 248°F, pour it over
the beaten eggs, beating slowly all the time. Increase the speed to high and
continue beating until the mixture cools. This will take a minimum of 7–8 minutes.

3
Using the electric whisk, beat the softened butter and gradually add the egg-syrup
mixture, as if making mayonnaise. Finally stir in the grated dark chocolate.

Decorating with chocolate
intense

☙❧

Chocolate decorations can be very varied; use flakes, scrolls, cut-outs, leaves, hearts, and many others to give a unique touch of elegance.

7 oz (200 g) 52% dark chocolate; or milk or white chocolate
Essential equipment: thermometer, waxed paper, spatula, palette knife,
silicone baking mat, holly leaf

Preparing the chocolate

Finely grate the chocolate into a bowl and melt it in a water bath or over a pan of water at a maximum temperature of 95°F. When the chocolate has melted, check the temperature; it should not exceed 89–91°F. Keep it at this temperature for 20 minutes, stirring from time to time, then transfer to a bowl. When the chocolate has cooled to 84–89°F, you can begin making your decorations.

❦

Flakes

To make flakes, you don't need to prepare the chocolate. Just chill the bar or slab in the refrigerator for 15 minutes, then grate it coarsely or finely.

❦

Scrolls

Pour the prepared chocolate over a work surface (ideally a marble slab) and spread it thinly. Before it has completely solidified, roll into scrolls with a metal palette knife.

❦

Cut-outs

Pour the prepared chocolate onto a sheet of waxed paper then spread into a thin, even layer. Leave to cool fully, if necessary by refrigerating for a while if the room is too warm. Next place the chocolate layer on another sheet of waxed paper and peel off the first one. Use a knife to cut out shapes of your choice: large or small rounds, squares, or triangles.

❦

Leaves

Put clean, smooth leaves (such as bay leaves) on the chocolate, without immersing them, then remove. Leave to cool for 15 minutes, then carefully peel off the chocolate. For more irregular leaves (holly leaves, for example), use a paintbrush to coat them with melted chocolate on one side only, then allow to cool before peeling off the chocolate leaf.

❦

Hearts

Cut out the required number of hearts in the required size or sizes from waxed paper. Lay on a non-stick sheet and paint with melted chocolate. Peel the heart shapes off the parchment when set.

Chocolate fudge
medium

∞∞

Everybody loves this sweet treat!

1 vanilla bean
1 cup heavy cream
1 cup superfine sugar
2 tablespoons honey
3½ oz (100 g) 70% dark chocolate, grated
2½ tablespoons unsalted butter
½ cup chopped almonds
½ cup chopped hazelnuts
Serves 6 · Preparation time: 25 minutes
Essential equipment: electric beater, sugar thermometer

1
Cut the vanilla bean open lengthwise with a small sharp knife.
Scrape out the seeds into a pan, and add the cream, sugar, honey,
vanilla bean, grated chocolate, and butter.

2
Bring the mixture to boiling point, then cook over a medium heat,
stirring frequently with a wooden spoon. Use a thermometer to check the
temperature and when it reaches 230–233°F, add the almonds and hazelnuts.

3
Bring to a boil again, then remove from the heat.
Pour the boiling mixture into a heatproof bowl and allow it to cool,
stirring constantly. Remove the vanilla bean. When the fudge thickens,
pour it into a mold and leave to harden then cut into squares.

Chocolate
mendiants
intense

∞∽

*These delicious confections are very easy
to make and perfect for coffee-breaks.*

8 oz (250 g) dark, white, or milk chocolate
1 cup mixed nuts, seeds and dried fruit (hazelnuts, walnuts,
pecans, sesame seeds, candied peel, crystallized ginger, raisins,
dried apricots, dried figs)
Makes around 20 mendiants · Preparation time: 25 minutes
Essential equipment: thermometer

1
Prepare the chocolate following the instructions on page 64.
2
Chop the nuts and dried fruits of your choice finely or otherwise, as you prefer.
Cover the work surface with two large sheets of waxed paper.
3
Using a tablespoon, spoon the chocolate onto the parchment,
making 20–25 fairly thin rounds (about ⅛ inch thick).
Sprinkle them with the fruit and nut mix as you go along.
4
Refrigerate the mendiants until set, then peel off the parchment.
They will keep for 4–5 days in an airtight box.

Variations
Go for a contrast by sprinkling some mendiants only with crystallized fruit and others
only with nuts. If you like sharp flavors, you might try seasoning them while still soft with
a pinch of Sichuan pepper, pimento, or allspice. You could also make bicolored ones
by using white and dark chocolate.

Chocolate candied orange strips
medium

⟢⟣

Candied orange-peel and chocolate make one of those great pairings that go naturally together, a bit like rum and raisins, for instance. Serve these orange strips at the end of dinner with a mellow Armagnac.

6 good-sized oranges
2½ pints cold water
8 lb superfine sugar
1 lb 52% dark chocolate, grated

Makes around 1½ lb orange strips · Preparation time: 1 hour
Cooking time: 1 hour · Macerating time: 6 days · Drying time: 1 day
Essential equipment: thermometer.

Remove the peel
Using a very sharp knife, peel the oranges, avoiding the pith and taking care not to pierce the flesh. Rinse the peel well and drain.
Plunge into a large pan of cold water, bring to a boil, and boil for 5 minutes before draining. Repeat this operation twice.

Candy the peel
Put the sugar and cold water in a pan and bring to a boil, stirring constantly. Add the blanched peel. Leave to cook over a very low heat for 1 hour. Skim with a small skimmer, then allow to cool completely.
Leave the peel and syrup mixture to macerate in the refrigerator for 6 days.

Prepare the peel
Drain the peel through a strainer. Cut into pencil-thin strips.
Spread out on a cookie sheet and leave to dry out in the kitchen for 24 hours.

Coating the peel
Prepare the chocolate following the instructions on page 64.
One by one, dip the strips of peel halfway into the chocolate then place them on waxed paper. Allow to cool and set for a while before serving.

Preparation tips
· The lengthy maceration or steeping in the syrup is essential to make sweet and well-candied peel. Do not speed it up.
· Once candied, the strips will keep for several months. They can be stored in the refrigerator and coated with chocolate only when you are ready to serve them.
· If the syrup begins to crystallize, add some water, bring back to a boil and allow to cool again.

Dark chocolate and Armagnac sabayon
subtle

∞ ∞

This light and elegant dessert is best served in thin-rimmed bowls or glasses. Serve it soon after cooking, as sabayon quickly loses its flavor if allowed to cool completely.

6 egg yolks
½ cup confectioners' sugar
4 tablespoons Armagnac
1 knob softened unsalted butter
1 tablespoon bitter cocoa
2 tablespoons chocolate flakes (see page 64)

Serves 4 · Preparation time: 35 minutes · Cooking time: 15 minutes
Essential equipment: electric beater

1

Put the egg yolks, confectioners' sugar, and Armagnac in a bowl and place in a water bath or over a pan of warm water. Beat the mixture with an electric whisk for around 15 minutes. When the mixture is well aerated and thick, add the butter. Remove the bowl from the pan and whip for another 12 minutes, away from the heat.

2

Divide the sabayon between four bowls and sift the cocoa over, using a fine-mesh strainer. Sprinkle with the chocolate flakes.

Chocolate rochers
intense

∞∞

Rochers are similar to truffles but with two differences:they are larger and they are covered with chocolate, not with cocoa powder. They are often flavored with almonds or hazelnuts.

1 cup peeled hazelnuts
11½ oz (350 g) 52% dark chocolate
Scant ½ cup thick crème fraîche
1½ tablespoons softened unsalted butter
10 oz (300 g) 70% dark chocolate, a single estate Jamaican one, if possible
Makes 10–12 rochers · Preparation time: 40 minutes · Resting time: 2 × 2 hours + 1 hour
Essential equipment: thermometer, broiler-rack

1
Chop the hazelnuts coarsely and toast in a pan for a few minutes.
Turn them out on a plate and allow to cool. Grate the two chocolates,
but do not mix them together. Melt the 52% chocolate in a water bath or a bowl
over a pan of hot water. Do not let the temperature go above 91°F.

2
Bring the crème fraîche to boiling point in a pan then remove from
the heat. Pour it over the melted chocolate, add the butter, and blend until it
becomes a shiny, thick mass. Add the hazelnuts.

3
Pour the chocolate-cream mixture into a dish lined with waxed paper,
cover with plastic wrap, and leave to cool in the refrigerator for around 2 hours.
You could also make the rochers by pouring the mixture into 5 × 1-inch flexible
molds. Chill in the refrigerator, unmold and continue to Step 5.

4
When the ganache is easily worked, make 10–12 rochers and
refrigerate for 2 hours. Meantime, prepare the 70% chocolate following
the instructions on page 64.

5
Using a fork, dip the rochers in the prepared chocolate and drain
them on a wire cooling rack. Leave in a cool place for
at least 1 hour before eating.

Variation
Try coating the rochers with milk chocolate and sprinkle them
with nuts while the chocolate is still soft.

Chocolate spread
medium

∽ ∾

*This chocolate spread makes a delicious snack for
children—and for adults! You can spread it on bread but it
can also be used as a filling for a jelly roll.*

½ cup ground praline (see below)
¾ cup heavy cream
1½ tablespoons unsalted butter
5 oz (150 g) milk chocolate, grated
3½ oz (100 g) 52% dark chocolate, grated
Makes 2 × 10 oz jars · Preparation time: 20 minutes · Resting time: 2 hours
Essential equipment: electric mixer

1
Put the ground praline, cream, and butter in a pan and bring to a boil. Remove from
the heat. Add the chocolates and blend until completely dissolved.

2
Pour the mixture into the mixing bowl and mix for 1 minute at maximum speed.

3
Pour this spread into jars; it will keep for a week in the refrigerator.

Ground praline
Heat 1⅓ cups unblanched almonds and ⅔ cup superfine sugar together in a pan.
Stir until sugar has caramelized to a golden brown, turn onto an
oiled baking sheet, and let cool. Grind to a powder
in a blender or food processor.

Waffles with chocolate
subtle

∞ ∞

The waffles can be flavored with a touch of vanilla and served with a chocolate sauce or you could add chocolate or cocoa directly to the batter.

½ cup butter
1 vanilla bean
⅓ cup sugar
2 eggs
2½ cups all-purpose flour
½ teaspoon baking powder
2 cups milk

Makes around 8 waffles · Preparation time: 15 minutes
Resting time: 15 minutes · Cooking time: 20 minutes
Essential equipment: waffle-maker

1

Melt the butter over a low heat and leave to cool. Cut the vanilla bean in half lengthwise and scrape out the seeds with the point of a knife.

2

Beat the sugar and the eggs together in a bowl. Sift in the flour and baking powder. Gradually beat in the milk until you have a fairly liquid batter. Finally, add the butter and the vanilla seeds.

3

Cook the waffles in a waffle-maker, and serve them while still warm with one of the sauces on page 120, the chocolate spread on page 76, one of the ganaches on page 57, or even a Chantilly cream flavored with a pinch of bitter cocoa.

Variation
Make the mix as shown opposite and add 4–4½ tablespoons sifted cocoa powder.

Chocolate roulade
medium

∽∾

To succeed with this great classic, don't overcook the sponge as it can become dry and difficult to roll. Here it is filled with a souffléd ganache but you could also use a buttercream filling, a Chantilly cream (whipped cream flavored with sugar and vanilla), or a coffee ganache.

Ingredients for the log
4 eggs, separated
⅔ cup superfine sugar
Scant cup all-purpose flour
1 tablespoon cocoa powder
2 tablespoons softened unsalted butter
2½ tablespoons milk
1 tablespoon confectioners' sugar
Salt
Serves 6–8 · Preparation time: 45 minutes
Resting time: 2 hours · Cooking time: 12 minutes
Essential equipment: cookie sheet, electric hand mixer

To make the log
Preheat the oven to 350°F. Put the yolks in a bowl, add the superfine sugar, and beat with the mixer until the mixture turns very pale and fluffy. Mix the flour and cocoa powder together and sift into the bowl. Finally add the butter and the milk. In a clean bowl whip the egg whites with a pinch of salt and the confectioners' sugar until stiff. Fold gently into the other mixture then spread evenly over a cookie sheet lined with waxed paper. Put in the oven for about 12 minutes, then remove and leave to cool for a few minutes.

The filling
Prepare the recipe for a plain or flavored souffléd ganache, following the instructions on page 57.

Finishing and decoration
Make chocolate flakes and scrolls following the instructions on page 64. Remove the waxed paper from the baked sponge. Spread the ganache over the whole surface (setting aside 2 tablespoonfuls for decoration), then carefully roll up, applying light pressure. When rolled, spread a thin coat of ganache over the top and sprinkle with flakes or scrolls of chocolate. Chill in the refrigerator for two hours before serving.

Black Forest gateau
medium

ᚼᚼ

*If you make a Black Forest gateau for children, don't use kirsch
in the syrup. This succulent cake should be eaten within
two hours of making, as the Chantilly cream is not very
stable and will quickly saturate the cake.*

1 chocolate Génoise (see recipe on page 86)
½ cup sugar
½ cup water
1½ tablespoons kirsch
1 vanilla bean
1¼ cups heavy cream, well-chilled
2 tablespoons confectioners' sugar
½ cup cherries, pitted
10 glacé cherries
Milk chocolate flakes, to decorate (see page 64)

Serves 6–8 · Preparation time: 45 minutes · Resting time: 2 hours · Cooking time: 25 minutes
Essential equipment: electric hand mixer, round cake rack

1
Make the chocolate Génoise as shown in the recipe on page 86.
Make a syrup by boiling the sugar with the water, then leave to cool. Add the
kirsch. When the Génoise has cooled, cut it into three even circles using
a long serrated-blade knife.

2
Slice the vanilla bean lengthwise and use a knife to scrape the seeds into a bowl.
To make a Chantilly cream, add the confectioners' sugar and the cream and beat
until stiff using the electric mixer.

3
Place one of the cake circles on a circular rack. Lightly moisten with the syrup.
Spread the Chantilly cream over and dot with fresh cherries. Put the second cake
circle on top and repeat the operation.

4
Finally place the third cake circle on top and cover with the remaining Chantilly
cream. Smooth the surface well, using a spatula, then decorate with the
glacé cherries and flakes of milk chocolate (see page 64).

Chocolate charlotte
intense

∞∞

This is the true chocoholic's favorite dessert.
There are many recipes but this one stands out for its
meltingly sensuous mousse.

For the mold
16–20 ladyfingers

For the charlotte
7 oz (200 g) 52% dark chocolate, grated
3½ oz (100 g) 70% dark chocolate,
a single estate Brazilian or Colombian, if possible
4 eggs, separated
1 tablespoon confectioners' sugar
1¾ cups heavy cream, well-chilled

Serves 6–8 · Preparation time: 1 hour · Resting time: overnight
Essential equipment: hand-held electric mixer, thermometer,
fluted charlotte mold approx 15 × 3½ inches in diameter

1
Arrange the ladyfingers around the charlotte mold and set aside.

2
Melt the chocolate in a water bath or in a bowl over a pan of warm
water. If possible, do not let the temperature exceed 91°F. Set aside.
Separate the eggs. In another, hotter water bath beat 4 egg whites and most
of the confectioners' sugar together, using an electric hand mixer at high speed.
Remove from the heat and beat for another 5 minutes until you have a pale,
aerated, and barely warm mixture. Set aside.

3
Beat 1 cup of the cream in a bowl into firm peaks. In another bowl whisk the
4 egg whites into peaks and fold in the remaining confectioners' sugar.

4
Bring the remaining cream to boiling point in a pan and add
to the melted chocolate. Stir well. When the mixture has thickened
slightly, add the egg yolks, egg white, and the whipped cream. Blend well and
fill the mold. Leave overnight in the refrigerator before unmolding.

Accompaniment
Serve the charlotte with one of the chocolate sauces on page 120.

Chocolate Génoise
medium

❧❧

A Génoise (from Genoa) is the basic recipe for many chocolate cakes.
It is equally delicious accompanied simply by a sauce, a ganache,
or a little Chantilly cream (see page 82, step 2).

1 cup all-purpose flour + extra for dusting
4 tablespoons cocoa powder
6 eggs
⅔ cup sugar
2 tablespoons unsalted butter + extra for greasing
Serves 6 · Preparation time: 20 minutes · Cooking time: 25–30 minutes
Essential equipment: electric hand mixer, round Génoise pan (or fluted flan pan)
10 inches in diameter

1
Preheat the oven to 350°F. Grease the baking pan and dust with flour, tapping
out the excess. Sift the flour and cocoa powder together. Put the eggs and
sugar in a bowl and use the mixer to beat for about 10 minutes until you have
a thick, ribbon-like consistency.

2
Add a quarter of the flour, cocoa, and melted butter, stirring carefully with
a spatula while rotating the bowl and retaining as much air as possible.
Continue with batches of flour, cocoa, and butter until it is all used.
(Do not incorporate the milky residue from the melted butter.)

3
Gently pour the batter into the prepared pan. Put in the preheated oven and
bake for 25–30 minutes. Leave in the pan for a few minutes before turning out the
still-warm Génoise onto a wire rack. Leave to cool for 25–30 minutes before eating
or using as the basis for another dessert.

Useful tip
Use extra-fresh organic eggs for this recipe to get a good consistency as they will fluff up better when beaten.

Chocolate gateau
intense

∞∞

½ cup unsalted butter
200 g (7 oz) dark chocolate, 52% or 64% cocoa content,
a Madagascar domain, if possible
⅔ cup superfine sugar
4 eggs
¾ cup all-purpose flour
Serves 6 · Preparation time: 25 minutes · Cooking time: 20–22 minutes
Essential equipment: Génoise or fluted round flan pan, about 8–9 inches in diameter

1
Preheat the oven to 350°F. Grease and flour a flan pan. Melt the butter and
the chocolate, broken up into small pieces, in a microwave or in a bowl over
a pan of warm water. Although the temperature reached by the melted chocolate
does not matter much in this recipe, do not let it overheat.

2
Put the sugar and eggs in a bowl then add the flour.

3
Add the melted chocolate-butter mixture to this and stir well to obtain
an even consistency.

4
Pour the mixture into the prepared flan pan. Put in the oven and bake for about
20 minutes. Remove from the oven and allow to cool for 10 minutes before
carefully turning out. Eat warm for preference.

Dark chocolate fondant
intense

∞∞

How do you make a successful chocolate pudding with a delicious runny center? The secret's in the cooking. While the pudding is in the oven in its mold, the heat penetrates gradually from the outside toward the center. In the case of runny centers, the exterior is cooked but the inside left almost raw. To achieve this, it is essential that there should be a sufficiently high difference in temperature between the pudding mixture and the oven, generally over 300°F.
This is called a temperature "gradient." For the runny center, this "gradient" needs to be high. For example, if the temperature of the mixture is 86°F, it should be cooked at 350°F. If there is not a sufficiently high difference (mixture at 95°F; oven at 300°F), the heat will penetrate more evenly, the center of the pudding will cook as much as the sides and will be solid, not runny, making a chocolate pudding but not a "melting middle" pudding.

7 oz (200 g) 52% dark chocolate,
a premium Asian one: Sri Lankan or Javanese, if possible
½ cup unsalted butter
4 eggs
¾ cup soft brown sugar
½ cup all-purpose flour
Salt

Serves 6 · Preparation time: 35 minutes · Cooking time: 10–12 minutes
Essential equipment: 8 individual molds 3 inches in diameter and 1½ inches deep

1
Preheat the oven to 350°F. Grease and flour the molds. Break up the chocolate and melt with the butter in a water bath, in a heatproof bowl over a pan of warm water, or in a microwave (at 160 watts for 3 minutes, or according to maker's instructions).

2
Beat the eggs and sugar in a bowl with a whisk. Add the flour while continuing to beat, then add a pinch of salt and the melted chocolate-butter mix. Blend well.

3
Pour the mixture into the prepared molds, put in the oven, and bake for 10–12 minutes. The time may vary by 2–3 minutes, depending on your oven. Remove from the oven and wait 5 minutes before turning out onto plates, then allow your guests to discover the marvelous sauce inside!

Chocolate marble cake
subtle

∞∞

*Another cake that's usually made for children
but which adults also enjoy.*

Scant cup superfine sugar
4 eggs
2⅔ cups all-purpose flour + extra for dusting
1 cup less 2 tablespoons unsalted butter + plus extra for greasing
1 cup ground almonds
½ cup heavy cream
2 teaspoons baking powder
2 tablespoons cocoa powder
Vanilla extract

Serves 6 · Preparation time: 35 minutes · Cooking time: 45–50 minutes
Essential equipment: 1 rectangular baking pan

Preparing the baking pan
Put the pan in the refrigerator for a good half-hour. Soften two knobs of butter
in your fingers and rub them over the inside, then dust with a tablespoonful
of flour, tapping out the excess.

Making the cake mix
Mix the sugar with the eggs. Add the flour, butter, almonds, cream, and
baking powder. Beat well to obtain a smooth mixture.

Flavoring the two mixtures
Separate the batter into two bowls. Add the cocoa powder to one and mix well.
Add a few drops of vanilla extract, to taste, to the other and stir in.

Molding and cooking
Preheat the oven to 325°F. Spread the vanilla mixture over the bottom of
the pan and smooth it out then pour the chocolate mixture on top without
touching the sides of the pan. Use a fork to mix the two very slightly. Put in the
oven and bake for 45–50 minutes. Insert a metal skewer to check that the cake
is done. Allow to cool then turn out of the pan.

Viennese hot chocolate
intense

◠◠

4 oz (120 g) 64% chocolate, a premier Central African brand, if possible
2 cups lowfat milk
2 tablespoons bitter cocoa + some for decoration
4 tablespoons superfine sugar
⅔ cup heavy cream, well-chilled
Serves 4 · Preparation time: 15 minutes
Essential equipment: electric hand blender or mixer

1
Grate the chocolate. Heat the milk, cocoa, and sugar in a pan.
2
Remove from the heat, add the grated chocolate and whisk the mixture at high
speed for at least 2 minutes. Beat the cream to firm peaks.
3
When the hot chocolate is very foamy, serve it immediately in large mugs, topped
with 2 tablespoons of the whipped cream. Sprinkle a little bitter cocoa over.

Variations
· Add the seeds of a vanilla bean to the whipped cream.
· To make an even richer Viennese chocolate, replace ⅓ cup of the milk with crème fraîche

Pound cake with cocoa
subtle

⟋⟍⟋⟍

1 cup unsalted butter
5 eggs
1 cup superfine sugar
2 cups all-purpose flour
2 teaspoons baking powder
5 tablespoons bitter cocoa

Serves 6–8 · Preparation time: 15 minutes · Cooking time: 35–40 minutes
Essential equipment: 2-lb loaf pan

1
Preheat the oven to 325°F. Grease and flour the baking pan.
Gently melt the butter in a pan without overheating.
Break the eggs into a bowl and beat for 1 minute
with the sugar. In another bowl sift together the flour,
baking powder, and cocoa.

2
Add the flour and cocoa blend to the egg-sugar mixture
and stir in, then add the melted butter and stir again.

3
Pour the mixture into the prepared pan, put in
the oven, and bake for 35–40 minutes.
Carefully unmold the cake while still hot
and leave to cool on a baking rack.
Eat warm for preference.

Butter-chocolate squares
subtle

∞∞

*At once melting and crunchy, these squares can be eaten at any time,
as soon as they are cooked. The pastry also makes a good base
for a delicious tart with roasted figs, pears, or prunes.*

4 tablespoons cocoa powder
2½ cups all-purpose flour
½ teaspoon baking powder
1½ cups confectioners' sugar
½ cup unsalted butter, softened + extra for greasing
6 tablespoons slightly-salted butter, softened
⅔ cup ground almonds
1 egg

Makes about 20 squares · Preparation time: 30 minutes · Cooking time: 25 minutes
Essential equipment: fine-mesh strainer, cookie sheet

The pastry
Preheat the oven to 325°F and grease a cookie sheet. Sift together the cocoa,
flour, and baking powder into a bowl. Add the sugar, the two kinds of
softened butter, and the ground almonds. Rub in, using your fingers or a
mixer until all the ingredients are fully incorporated. The mixture should be
floury and will look a bit like a crumble.

Shaping the squares
Set aside one quarter of the mixture. Add the egg to the remainder and mix
in to make a compact ball. Turn out on the buttered cookie sheet and flatten
with your palm to a thickness of ⅜–¾ inch. Put the remaining quarter
on top and press down with the flat of your hand to make it stick firmly.

Cooking
Cut the pastry into squares or rectangles with a knife to whatever size you prefer.
Place them on the cookie sheet, put in the oven, and bake for about 20 minutes.
Allow to cool slightly on a wire rack then serve in a dish or plate.

Useful tips
· The first dough layer should be well pressed down, but it's enough to make sure that the second one
adheres to it—it's the difference in texture between the two layers that makes this recipe so appealing.
· Instead of cutting squares, use cookie cutters to make small individual shapes of your choice.

Chocolate macaroons
medium

∞∞∞

Served plain or filled with a ganache,
these macaroons are irresistible and unbeatable.

1 cup ground almonds
1¾ cups confectioners' sugar
3 tablespoons bitter cocoa
½ cup egg whites
4 tablespoons superfine sugar

Makes about 20 macaroons · Preparation time: 20 minutes
Cooking time: 12–15 minutes
Essential equipment: electric mixer, electric whisk,
cookie sheet, waxed paper, pastry bag

1
Preheat the oven to 325°F and line a cookie sheet with waxed paper.
Put the ground almonds, confectioners' sugar, and cocoa in the mixer bowl
and mix at high speed for 1 minute.

2
Beat the egg whites into stiff peaks, then add the superfine sugar. Beat for
another minute. Add the almond mixture and stir in lightly. The egg whites
should collapse slightly and the mixture should form a "ribbon" when poured
from a wooden spoon.

3
Fill the pastry bag with the mixture (no need for a piping tip). Pipe about
20 macaroons onto the cookie sheet, spacing them evenly. Put in the oven
and bake for 12–15 minutes. Allow to cool, then gently detach the macaroons
from the lining paper.

Useful tips
To ensure the macaroons have a smooth, shiny exterior, the mixture should not be too light.
This is why the beaten egg white should be encouraged to collapse slightly when you
incorporate the almonds, confectioners' sugar, and cocoa.

Big chocolate brownie
intens

∞ ∞

This chocolate brownie should not be turned out, so bake it in a pretty dish that you can bring to the table.

7 oz (200 g) 52% or 70% dark chocolate,
a premium brand from the Dominican Republic, if possible

½ cup supe
½ cup + 1 tablespoon unsalted
Scant ⅓ cup all-purpose flou
1½ tablespoons ground almonds
Ground cinnamon
1 cup walnuts, roughly chopped

Serves about 6 · Preparation time: 20 minutes · Cooking time: 20–25 minutes · Resting Time: 2 hours
Essential equipment: 6-inch square (ideally) ovenproof dish

1

Preheat the oven to 350°F. Grease the baking pan and line the base with
waxed paper. Break up the chocolate and melt gently in a water bath,
or in a bowl over a pan of warm water, without overheating, although accurate
temperature control is not necessary for this recipe.

2

Break the eggs into a bowl and stir in the sugar. Fold in the softened butter,
flour, almonds, 2 pinches of ground cinnamon, the melted chocolate, and
finally the chopped walnuts.

3

Pour the mixture into the baking dish, put in the oven, and bake for 20–25 minutes.
Allow to cool for two hours before eating.

Variation
Replace the walnuts with pecans, macadamia, hazelnuts, almonds, or a mixture of all of these.

Choc-chip cookies
intense

∞∞

In this American recipe, chocolate buttons or small chips of chocolate are added to the dough, without mixing in, to make deliciously contrasting tastes, colors, and textures.

½ cup unsalted butter
¾ cup confectioners' sugar
1 vanilla bean
1 egg
1 cup + 1 tablespoon all-purpose flour
1⅓ cups ground almonds
3 oz (80 g) 70% dark chocolate
Salt
Makes 15–20 cookies · Preparation time: 20 minutes
Cooking time: 8 minutes · Resting time: 30 minutes
Essential equipment: cookie sheet

1
Leave the butter at room temperature until it softens, or put briefly in the microwave, taking care it does not melt. Put the sugar in a bowl and mix in the softened butter. Slice the vanilla bean in half lengthwise. Use a knife to scrape out the seeds into the butter-sugar mix.

2
Add the egg and mix again, fold in the flour, almonds, and a pinch of salt. Work the dough until you obtain an even consistency. Leave to rest for 30 minutes.

3
Preheat the oven to 350°F. Grease a cookie sheet. Chop the dark chocolate into fairly uniform chips with a knife.

4
Use a spoon to drop small balls of dough about the size of a large walnut on the cookie sheet, spacing them evenly. Flatten them with a fork dipped in water then sprinkle with small chocolate chips, pressing them into the dough with the palm of the hand. Cook for 8 minutes then remove from the cookie sheet with a metal spatula and leave to cool.

Chocolate dacquoises
subtle

∽∾

*This recipe is similar to that for macaroons but the use of
hazelnuts instead of almonds completely alters the taste and texture.
Dacquoises can be eaten plain or with a ganache filling.*

1⅓ cups ground hazelnuts
1¼ cups confectioners' sugar + extra for decoration
4 tablespoons bitter cocoa powder
4 egg whites
4 tablespoons superfine sugar
½ cup chopped hazelnuts

Makes about 20 dacquoises · Preparation time: 20 minutes · Cooking time: 10–12 minutes
Essential equipment: mixer, electric whisk, cookie sheet, waxed paper, pastry bag

1
Preheat the oven to 325°F. Line the cookie sheet with
waxed paper. Assemble the ground hazelnuts, confectioners'
sugar, and cocoa in the mixing bowl and whizz at high
speed for a few seconds.

2
Whisk the egg whites to form soft peaks then add
the superfine sugar and whisk for another minute.
Fold in the hazelnut-sugar-cocoa mixture. The egg whites
should collapse slightly and the meringue should be ribbon-like.

3
Put the mixture in the pastry bag (no need for a piping tip) and pipe
20 or so dacquoises, spacing them evenly on the cookie sheet.
Sprinkle with chopped hazelnuts, put in the oven, and bake for 10–12 minutes.
Allow to cool then peel carefully off the cookie sheet and sprinkle
with confectioners' sugar.

Chocolate madeleines
subtle

Madeleines are small, scallop-shaped cakes, an afternoon teatime favorite in France. They go well with chocolate flavoring. Try adding bitter cocoa to the batter or sprinkling the tops with chocolate flakes before cooking. You could even make two different batches of batter, cooking them together like a marble cake.

½ cup unsalted butter + extra for greasing
1½ oz (30 g) 52% dark chocolate
3 eggs
Scant ¾ cup sugar
1 cup + 1 tablespoon all-purpose flour + extra for dusting
½ teaspoon baking powder
Vanilla extract

Makes 20–25 madeleines · Preparation time: 15 minutes
Resting time: 15 minutes · Cooking time: 10 minutes
Essential equipment: madeleine pan(s) are preferable but cupcake pans will do

1
Preheat the oven to 350°F. Grease the baking pans
and dust with flour, tapping to remove excess. Melt the butter
over a low heat then let it cool. Grate the chocolate
and melt it in a water bath or in a bowl over a pan of warm
water, taking care not to overheat. Set aside..

2
Use a hand whisk to beat the eggs and sugar together for 20 seconds.
Add the flour, baking powder, and a few drops of vanilla essence and
whisk a bit more. Finally add the melted butter. Divide the batter in
two parts and add the melted chocolate to one.

3
Fill the baking pans three-quarters full with the white batter,
then with the chocolate one. Leave to rest for 15 minutes before
putting in the oven and baking for 10 minutes.

Chocolate éclairs
medium

∞∞

*This absolutely classic chocolate patisserie is delicious
when home-made, especially when eaten an hour after cooking.
A great dessert to rediscover.*

The choux pastry
1 cup unsalted butter
250 ml (8 fl oz) water
½ tablespoon sugar
1 cup all-purpose flour
4 eggs
Salt

Makes 16 éclairs · Preparation time: 1 hour
Resting time: 1 hour · Cooking time: 35 minutes
Essential equipment: pastry bag with a piping tip

Preheat the oven to 400°F. Grease and flour a cookie sheet. Put the butter,
water, sugar, and a pinch of salt in a pan and gently bring to a boil.
Remove from the heat when the mixture reaches boiling point. Add the flour
and mix in vigorously. When the pastry is quite thick, add the eggs one by one,
beating all the time. Place the dough in the pastry bag and pipe 16 éclairs
onto the cookie sheet, spacing them evenly. Put in the oven and bake for
35 minutes then leave to cool on a wire rack.

The chocolate custard cream
Prepare the chocolate custard cream filling following the
instructions on page 61. Allow it to cool. When you are ready to fill the éclairs,
work it for 1 minute with a spoon to make it supple.

Finishing
Make an incision lengthwise along each éclair and fill with the chocolate
custard cream, using either a spoon or a pastry bag.

Glazing
10 oz fondant
2 tablespoons bitter cocoa

In a pan over low heat, melt the fondant and bitter cocoa gently,
blending well. Dip the top of each éclair into the chocolate mix, wiping off the
excess with your finger. Wait at least an hour before eating.

Useful tips
· Never boil the fondant as it will lose its glossiness.
· You can buy fondant in the baking departments of supermarkets.
· If you cannot find fondant, dip the éclairs in a little melted chocolate.

Chocolate profiteroles
medium

∞∞

Made with choux pastry and home-made vanilla ice cream, this great classic is simply irresistible. The pastry shells can be made in advance and kept in the freezer but when filled with ice cream they should be eaten within the day otherwise they will go soggy.

The vanilla ice cream
2 vanilla beans
1 cup milk
1 cup cream
5 egg yolks
⅔ cup superfine sugar

The choux pastry
1 quantity of choux pastry (see the recipe on page 111)
1 egg, beaten

The garnish
½ cup slivered almonds, toasted
2 tablespoons confectioners' sugar

The sauce
½ cup milk
5 oz (150 g) 52% or 70% dark chocolate, chopped
Makes around 30 profiteroles · Preparation time: 1 hour
Resting time: 1 + 2 hours · Cooking time: about 30 minutes
Essential equipment: ice-cream maker

The ice cream
Cut the vanilla beans in half lengthwise and scoop out the seeds, using the point of a knife. In a pan, bring the milk, cream, vanilla beans, and their seeds to simmering point. Whisk the mixture then remove the pan from the heat and leave it, covered, to infuse for 15 minutes. Beat the egg yolks and sugar in a bowl for 1 minute then add the vanilla-flavored milk. Mix well, return the mixture to a pan, and cook until it thickens into a light custard. Take the pan off the heat, strain the mixture through a fine sieve, and leave to cool. Discard the vanilla beans.

The choux buns
Make the choux pastry following the recipe on page 111, then pipe out 30 or so small buns onto a cookie sheet. Glaze with beaten egg, put in the oven, and bake for 25–30 minutes at 350°F. Allow to cool then remove from the cookie sheet and freeze for 1 hour.

The filling
Meanwhile, put the vanilla cream in the ice-cream maker. When the ice-cream is fairly thick, fill the buns, using a spoon or a pastry bag with a tip, then return to the freezer for at least 2 hours.

The sauce and decoration
Toast the almonds in a pan with the confectioners' sugar and set aside. Make the sauce just before you plan to serve: bring the milk to simmering point in a pan, remove from the heat, and add the chocolate, stirring it to melt in. Arrange the profiteroles on plates, pour the chocolate sauce over, and sprinkle with the toasted almonds. Serve immediately.

Chocolate fondue
medium

∽∾

This "children's special" is easy to make and always appreciated.

1½ oz (30 g) 52% dark chocolate
2 oz (50 g) white chocolate
8 oz (250 g) milk chocolate
1¾ cups milk
3 tablespoons cornstarch
1 brioche (available in bakeries and supermarkets)
2 bananas
Serves about 8, perhaps with some leftover ingredients for another time
Preparation time: 30 minutes
Essential equipment: fondue set

1
Break up the chocolates then melt in a water bath, or in a bowl over
a pan of warm water, stirring occasionally. Meantime, put the milk and
cornstarch in a pan and whisk to blend, then boil briefly, whisking all the
time, before removing from the heat. Pour the mixture over the melted
chocolate. Stir with a wooden spoon to obtain a smooth, creamy consistency.
2
Pour this mixture into the fondue dish. Make sure that the chocolate
stays hot but does not boil.
3
Cut the brioche into small cubes and put them in a bowl. Peel and chop
the bananas, then let the children dip the brioche cubes and banana slices
in the chocolate using fondue forks or wooden chopsticks—under
strict supervision, of course!

Hot chocolate soufflé
medium

∽∽

*Like all hot soufflés, this recipe is a bit demanding as it needs
to be made at the last minute, but it's well worth it.*

Butter and superfine sugar for the soufflé dishes
6 oz (175 g) 64% dark chocolate
½ cup heavy cream
2 tablespoons bitter cocoa powder
5 egg whites
½ cup confectioners' sugar
4 egg whites
Makes 4 individual soufflés · Preparation time: 25 minutes · Cooking time: 15 minutes
Essential equipment: individual soufflé dishes, electric whisk

1

Preheat the oven to 400°F. Butter the soufflé dishes and coat with sugar.
Grate the chocolate and melt in a water bath or a bowl over a pan
of warm water. Bring the cream to boiling point in a pan then add the
melted chocolate and the cocoa powder. Blend well to make a fairly thick mixture.

2

Whisk the egg whites into firm peaks, add the confectioners' sugar, and whisk
again for one minute. Beat the egg yolks into the chocolate mixture, then gently
fold in the egg whites (first folding in 3–4 tablespoons, then the remainder).

3

Fill the soufflé dishes with the mixture, smoothing the surface with a palette knife.
Put in the oven for 12–15 minutes then serve immediately.

Iced chocolate soufflé
medium

∽∾

To be made 1 or 2 days in advance, in individual dishes.
This recipe is quite tricky, as it involves making a sabayon,
but an electric whisk helps a lot.

The sabayon
5 egg yolks
½ cup superfine sugar
Knob of butter, softened

The other ingredients
7 oz (200 g) 52% or 70% dark chocolate
½ cup heavy cream
4½ tablespoons bitter cocoa powder
5 egg whites
½ cup confectioners' sugar
Makes 4 individual soufflés · Preparation time: 45 minutes · Resting time: 24 hours
Essential equipment: individual soufflé dishes, electric whisk, waxed paper

1
Cut 4 strips of waxed paper, each 6 inches (or circumference of the
dish) × 2½ inches. Wrap them around the outside of the soufflé dishes and hold
in place with an elastic band. The paper should be 1 inch higher than the top
of each dish. Make the sabayon: put the egg yolks, superfine sugar, and
3 tablespoons of water in a bowl. Put this in a water bath or in a bowl set over
a pan of fairly hot water and whisk the mixture for around 15 minutes.
When it is well-aerated and quite thick, add the butter. Remove the bowl from the
heat and whisk again for 12 minutes while it cools. Set aside.

2
Grate the chocolate and melt it in a warm water bath. Bring the cream to boiling
point in a pan, then add the melted chocolate and the cocoa powder.
Blend well to make a fairly thick mixture.

3
Beat the egg whites into stiff peaks then fold in the confectioners' sugar,
little by little, beating all the time for 3 minutes. Fold the sabayon mixture and
the egg whites into the chocolate.

4
Fill the soufflé dishes and freeze them for at least 24 hours. Remove the waxed
paper just before serving the iced soufflés.

Accompaniment
Serve your iced soufflés with one of the sauces on page 120.

Chocolate sauces
intense

୧୦ଡ଼ଡ଼

*Served hot, warm, or cold, chocolate sauce is
the natural accompaniment to many desserts.
Don't forget this essential finishing touch.*

Dark chocolate sauce to be served hot

1¼ cups whole milk
2 tablespoons cornstarch
10 oz (300 g) 52% dark chocolate, grated,
a Venezuelan domain, if possible

Serves 6 · Preparation time: 5 minutes

Put the milk and cornflour in a pan and beat together over a medium heat,
using a hand whisk. Whisk until the mixture thickens slightly then take off the
heat. Add the grated chocolate and stir until it has completely dissolved.
Serve immediately.

❦

Milk chocolate sauce to be served warm

1 cup whole milk
Seeds from ½ vanilla bean
2½ oz (60 g) milk chocolate, grated
1¼ oz (30 g) dark chocolate, grated
2 tablespoons confectioners' sugar
2 egg whites
½ teaspoon cornflour

Serves 4 · Preparation time: 15 minutes

1
Use a hand whisk to beat the milk and vanilla seeds over a low or medium heat,
then add both kinds of chocolate. Whisk the confectioners' sugar and egg whites
in a bowl and fold in the cornstarch.

2
Pour the chocolate-milk mixture over the sugar-eggs mixture and transfer
the lot to a pan. Bring to simmering point, stirring constantly, then remove from
the heat. Serve warm.

❦

Chocolate sauce to be served cold

1 cup whole milk
2 tablespoons bitter cocoa powder
4 tablespoons superfine sugar
2 egg yolks

Serves 4 · Preparation time: 15 minutes

Whisk the milk and cocoa powder together, beating constantly.
Whisk the sugar and egg yolks together in a bowl, then pour over the milk
and cocoa mixture, stir well and pour into a pan. Cook over a moderate
heat, stirring slowly and continuously with a wooden spoon, until the mixture
thickens just enough to coat the spoon lightly. Strain through a fine-mesh
strainer and leave to cool completely. Serve cold or chilled.

White chocolate mousse
subtle

ᗌᗌ

This mousse can be served on its own but it can also be used to fill a Génoise, a jelly roll, or profiteroles.

4 egg yolks
1½ tablespoons superfine sugar
10 oz (300 g) white chocolate, grated
6 tablespoons unsalted butter
2 cups heavy cream, well chilled
Serves 6–8 · Preparation time: 35 minutes · Resting time: 3 hours
Essential equipment: electric beater

1
Put the egg yolks, superfine sugar, and 3 tablespoons of cold water in a bowl. Place the bowl over a fairly hot water bath or double pan and whisk the mixture with an electric beater for about 15 minutes. When the mass is well-aerated and quite thick, remove the bowl from the water bath and whisk again for 12 minutes while it cools.

2
Melt the white chocolate in a metal bowl over a double pan filled with warm water, stirring occasionally with a wooden spoon. Melt the butter separately, taking care not to let it get too hot, then pour over the chocolate and blend in.

3
Whisk the heavy cream in a bowl until very firm. Add the beaten egg yolks to the melted chocolate-butter mixture, then fold in the cream. Leave to set in the refrigerator for at least 3 hours.

Attention
Check your ice-cream maker's maximum capacity carefully.
If necessary, reduce the quantities in this recipe by one-third or half.

Chocolate ice cream
intense

∞∞

*Ideally this chocolate ice cream should be served as soon
as you take it out of the ice-cream maker. It is absolutely delicious
when it is meltingly fresh.*

2 cups milk
2 cups heavy cream
5 tablespoons bitter cocoa powder
7 oz (200 g) 64% dark chocolate, a single origin South American one, if possible
8 egg yolks
½ cup superfine sugar

Serves 6–8 · Preparation time: 35 minutes · Cooking time: 10 minutes · Resting time: 2 hours
Essential equipment: ice-cream maker

1
Put the milk and heavy cream in a pan, add the bitter cocoa
and broken-up chocolate, and whisk briefly. Bring to simmering point
over a moderate heat, then remove from the heat. Make sure that the
chocolate and cocoa have melted fully and there are no lumps.

2
Beat the egg yolks and sugar together in a metal bowl until the mixture
turns very pale. Add the chocolate-milk mixture, whisking all the time,
then pour into a pan.

3
Cook over a low heat for around 10 minutes, stirring constantly with a wooden
spoon, until the mixture thickens just enough to coat the spoon lightly.

4
When the sauce has thickened, remove the pan from the heat.
Strain the sauce using a fine-mesh strainer. Leave it to cool completely.
Allow at least 2 hours before putting it in the ice-cream maker.
Serve immediately it reaches the right consistency.

Chocolate truffles
intense

∞∞

*Make these chocolate truffles with a butter ganache,
as it will melt deliciously. The flavors can be varied
by using dark chocolate of different cocoa content.
Use bitter cocoa power to coat the truffles.
See page 57 for other ganache recipes.*

7 oz (200 g) 64% dark chocolate, a premium Costa Rican brand, if possible
5 oz (150 g) 52% dark chocolate
⅔ cup thick crème fraîche
4 tablespoons unsalted butter, softened and cut into small pieces
7 oz (200 g) bitter cocoa powder
Makes 40–50 truffles · Preparation time: 40 minutes · Resting time: 3 hours
Essential equipment: strainer

1
Grate the dark chocolate finely. Bring the crème fraîche to boiling point in
a pan then remove from the heat and add the grated chocolate.
Add the butter and mix together until all the ingredients have blended to
a thick, glossy mass.

2
Transfer the ganache to a dish lined with waxed paper, cover with plastic wrap,
and refrigerate for around 3 hours.

3
Turn out the solidified ganache then roll it into small balls or cut into squares,
rectangles, or triangles, as you prefer.

4
Sift the cocoa powder into a dish and use a fork to roll the truffles in it
without touching them with your fingers. Shake off any excess cocoa then
put the truffles on a plate or in little dishes. Store in the refrigerator until
they are to be eaten.

Variations
Give your truffles a unique flavor by infusing the crème fraîche with a pinch of chili powder, to taste.
Other flavorings to personalize your truffles include jasmine tea, Sichuan pepper, or star anise.

Hot chocolate
intense

⬡⬡

4 oz (120 g) 70% dark chocolate, Javanese if possible
2 cups lowfat milk
4 tablespoons bitter cocoa powder + some for serving
2½ tablespoons superfine sugar
Serves 4 · Preparation time: 15 minutes
Essential equipment: hand-held mixer or whisk

1
Grate the chocolate and set aside.
Heat the milk, cocoa, and sugar in a pan.
2
Away from the heat, add the chocolate and whisk
the mixture at high speed for at least 2 minutes.
3
When the hot chocolate is very frothy, serve immediately
in four large cups. Sprinkle over some cocoa powder.

Variation
For true chocolate-lovers, replace the milk with mineral water.
This will make the drink less rich and frothy but the chocolate flavor
will be much more intense.

Chocolate tart
medium

∽∞∽

*This superb dessert is made by simply pairing sweet pastry
with ganache. Chocolate with a high cocoa content makes the tart
quite sharp, while milk chocolate will sweeten it.*

The pastry
½ cup unsalted butter, softened + extra for greasing
3 tablespoons confectioners' sugar
⅓ cup ground almonds
1⅓ cups all-purpose flour + extra for dusting
1 egg yolk
Serves 6–8 · Preparation time: 40 minutes
Resting time: 2 × 1 hours · Cooking time: 20 minutes
Essential equipment: flan ring 8–10 inches in diameter

1
Mix together the butter, confectioners' sugar, ground almonds, and flour in a bowl,
or directly on a pastry board. Add the egg yolk, knead well, and form into a ball.
Wrap and chill in the refrigerator for 1 hour.

2
Preheat the oven to 400°F. Butter and flour the flan ring. Press the pastry
into the ring and push above the edge to make an even rim of dough all around.
Line the pastry with waxed paper weighted with a handful of dried beans or
pie weights and bake blind for 20 minutes. Remove from the oven, allow to
cool then remove the paper and the beans.

The chocolate filling
11½ oz (350 g) chocolate (dark or milk),
a premium brand from Sao Tomé, if possible
¾ cup crème fraîche

1
Grate the chocolate coarsely or chop it into chunks. Bring the crème fraîche
to boiling point then immediately remove from the heat. Add the chocolate
and blend well, away from the heat.

2
When the mixture has formed a smooth, glossy, and still rather liquid mass,
pour it evenly into the pastry shell. Allow to cool then chill in the refrigerator
for 1 hour. Serve chilled.

Useful tips
· Decorate your tart with nuts. Chop almonds, pistachios, and hazelnuts, toast them in a pan with a pinch of
confectioners' sugar and sprinkle over the tart when the chocolate filling has hardened slightly.
· Dessert chocolate with praline would be perfect in this recipe.
· To make sure the chocolate tart is quite smooth, pour the filling into the shell while still hot,
so that it spreads well. Do not smooth it with a spoon or spatula, as they will leave traces.
· Here is a good combination of dark chocolate for the filling: 7 oz (200 g) of 52% cocoa content,
3½ oz (100 g) of 64% and 2 oz (50 g) of 70%.

Iced chocolate
intense

∞∞

4 oz (120 g) 52% dark chocolate
2 cups mineral water
4½ tablespoons bitter cocoa powder + some for sprinkling
4 tablespoons superfine sugar
Serves 4 · Preparation time: 15 minutes
Essential equipment: hand blender or whisk

1
Grate the chocolate. Bring the mineral water, cocoa powder,
and sugar to simmering point in a pan.

2
Away from the heat, add the chocolate and blend at high speed
for at least 2 minutes.

3
When the hot chocolate is frothy, leave it to cool for a while, then serve
in glasses half-full of ice-cubes. Sprinkle over some cocoa powder.

Chocolate around the world

The whole world appreciates chocolate; it seems that gourmets
everywhere like the same things, and often on the same occasions,
since chocolate consumption "peaks" at Easter and Christmas,
not just in Europe but also in the United States and, to a lesser degree,
in Japan, where chocoholics know how to make themselves heard.

In the United States, the famous Hershey's™ brand, originating in Pennsylvania,
has catered to gourmets for over a century. This well-known company
has constructed a veritable empire, with schools and crèches for its employees,
training establishments, stores, and even a museum—of chocolate, naturally!

In Japan some talented chocolate-makers have opened superb boutiques,
managing to conquer a sophisticated and demanding clientele.
Their creations are influenced by Japanese culture, and include confectionery
with flowers, in sushi shapes, and many others.

In China, a chocolate tradition barely exists but a newly prosperous,
urban class is willing to be persuaded. In June 2005 a large Chocolate Salon
was held in Beijing and an appreciative public discovered ganaches,
confectionery, mousses, and many other delicacies with great enthusiasm.

However, Mexico, where chocolate originated, is still the place where
the chocolate tradition flourishes as it were in a family setting, without fanfare.
Tejate, a specialty of Oaxaca State, is a delicious iced drink made from maize,
flor de cacao, fermented cocoa beans, water, sugar—
and a touch of charred wood.

Champurado is another drink, this time served hot and flavored with cinnamon
and *piloncillo*, unrefined cane sugar.

As for *moles*, these famous Mexican sauces come powdered or as a paste
and are used alone or as a basis for other sauces. Colors range from dark brown
to orange-red, depending on ingredients and the amount of chiles used.
All contain bitter cocoa and are a splendid accompaniment to chicken or turkey.

The iconic "chocolate" festivals

Easter

Easter is the supreme chocolate feast, when the greatest variety of shapes comes to the fore. The Easter egg, so intrinsic to this festival, is made in many sizes. The tradition of giving eggs goes back many centuries; in France, for instance, Louis XIV would bless great baskets of gilded eggs, which he gave to his courtiers and servants to thank them for their services. Traditionally the king himself received the biggest egg in the kingdom.

Nowadays children get the eggs, to their great delight. It seems that the origin of Easter eggs dates from the establishment of Lent. The Church forbade eggs to be eaten for 40 days and so, when the period of fasting had ended, in order not to waste the eggs that had accumulated during that time the most recent ones were cooked or conserved and the older ones were boiled and decorated.

The custom of painting and decorating eggs is still very strong in the Ukraine and in most Slavic countries. It is traditional to give them to family and friends on Easter day, with the greeting "Christ has risen!". In Alsace, Germany, Switzerland, and Austria, Easter eggs are said to be brought by the Easter bunny (*Oesterhase*). This is why chocolate rabbits are also made, along with bells, hens, and chickens in all kinds of shapes and sizes.

Christmas

Chocolate plays a big part at Christmas, with small or large
Santa Claus figures and chocolate balls and other shapes used to
decorate the branches of the Christmas tree. Gifts of specialty boxes
of chocolates are also an important feature of the feast.

☙

Children delight in an Advent calendar with little windows to be
opened each day revealing milk chocolate squares inside.
Advent (from the Latin word *adventus* meaning "coming") is the
four-week period preceding Christmas. It begins on the fourth Sunday
before Christmas and marks the start of the ecclesiastical year.
The Advent calendar developed from a Germanic tradition designed
to teach children patience. Originally, a pious image was put in the
window each morning, bearing a verse from the Gospels.
Later, cookies or chocolates took the place of these images and the
calendar then became a piece of card with 24 windows, one to be opened
every day and each containing a chocolate. Sometimes a Gospel verse
is also included. Christmas is also the time for confectionery,
truffles, and other delicacies to accompany or conclude festive meals.

☙

The tradition of the Christmas log is linked to the celebration of the
winter solstice. On Christmas Eve, it was customary to burn a log in
the hearth, one large enough to last for the 12 days of the festival.
Wood from fruit trees was preferred as a guarantee of fertile harvests
during the coming year. The log was sometimes blessed with a branch
of boxwood, which was then kept until Palm Sunday.

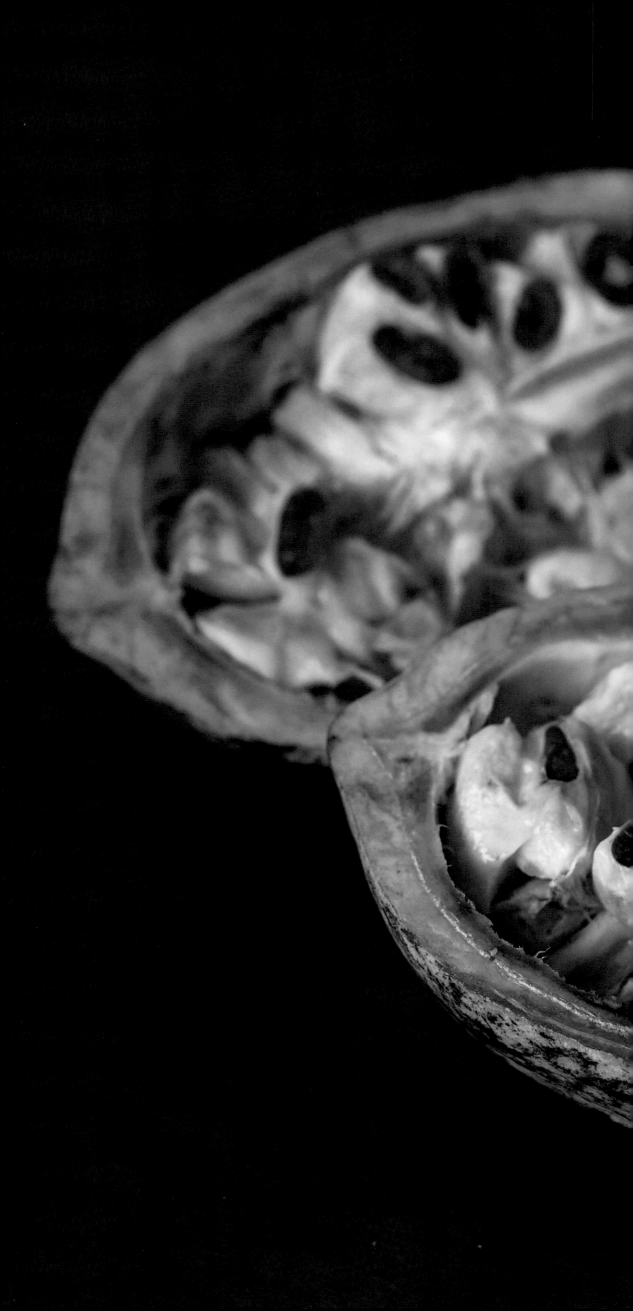

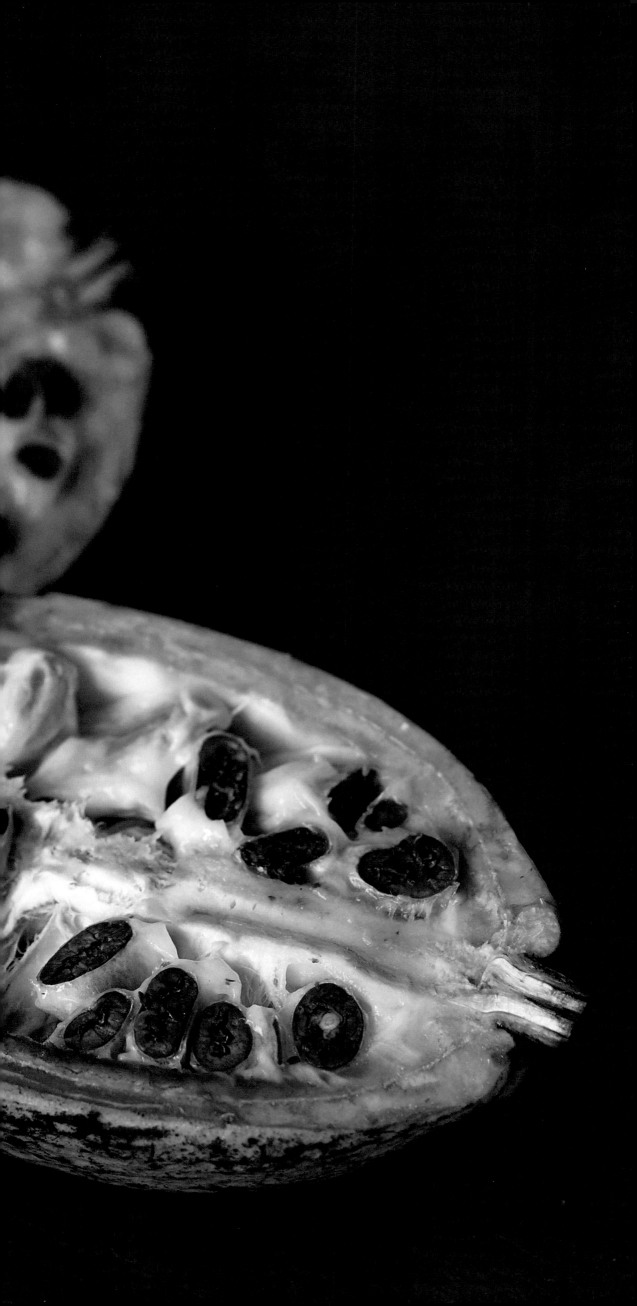

MORE ABOUT CHOCOLATE

BUYING WITH CONFIDENCE

*It's not always easy to make a choice when buying chocolate:
there is such a range. Here are a few tips to help you..*

Big supermarkets or
specialist chocolate-makers?

It's difficult to be specific because some very good "commercial" chocolate
exists. The chief advantage of a specialist seller is the advice you will get.
Complex recipes such as those for bouchées, truffles, or ones containing
spices, flavorings, or flowers require great skill and are definitely more
authentic when they are made by specialists, known as "chocolatiers."

The ideal "chocolate
store cupboard"

Whether for cooking or for eating alone, it is always good to have
the widest possible choice of chocolates. Always keep a supply of several
dark chocolates to form the core of your range. Choose chocolates
with a cocoa content of 52%, 70%, 80%, or even 99%, which are now
becoming more readily available and also by mail order.

∞∞

Look for chocolates that are designated PGI (Protected Geographical
Indication), meaning exceptional products coming from specified regions
that give them their particular character: each plantation, each production
hacienda has its own unique characteristics. Increasingly, chocolates
are made organically or come from Fairtrade cooperatives such as
Kuapa Kokoo from Ghana or Bolivia's El Ceibo.

∞∞

Don't overlook milk chocolates. High-quality milk chocolate can now be
found alongside standard products and there are some absolutely delicious
premium brands. There are also some milk chocolates that have undergone
a high degree of grinding and refining (see page 155). The cocoa particles
are so fine that the product achieves a unique texture and melting quality.
Keep several brands to hand as each has its own characteristics.

∞∞

When buying white chocolate, go for well-known brands.
Ideally, these will also come from specialist chocolate-makers.
Check the quality of cocoa powders and select only high quality products.
Do not confuse them with sugared drinking chocolate powders,
which are nothing like and are not used in the same way.

Useful tips
The list of ingredients may indicate the amount of vegetable fat, other than cocoa butter,
which has been added, possibly to lower the price. Be wary if this exceeds 5%.

TIPS AND TRICKS
WHEN COOKING CHOCOLATE

Melting the chocolate

Whichever method you choose—in a water bath, a microwave, or in a bowl over a saucepan of simmering water—chocolate should never be overheated when melting. Remember that the melting point of cocoa butter is approximately 86°F. Overheating destroys chocolate's structure, although this may not be obvious to the naked eye. Take care and make sure that the bowl used for melting is perfectly dry.

Add the ingredients
to the melted chocolate

Always begin by adding the butter or cream, followed by the egg yolks, if required in the recipe. Remember that chocolate is an emulsion and is therefore very sensitive to water (even if this comes from the egg yolks), which may cause it to seize or turn into an unworkable solid ball.

Making a ganache

The more chocolate is grated, broken up, or chopped, the quicker it will dissolve, with less risk of lumps. The principle is simple, try to stick to it.

Incorporate beaten egg whites
in a mousse

Always minimize the mixing time: the more you stir while incorporating the egg whites, the quicker they will lose their micro-bubbles of air.

Allow a chocolate cake to cool

Unmold it and leave to cool on a baking rack so that escaping steam can dissipate without softening the cake.

Using bitter cocoa powder

Always take the time to sift it through a fine-mesh strainer as it tends to settle and go lumpy during storage.

Useful tips
Remember that bitter cocoa powder and all dark chocolates contain theobromina, an alkaline to which some people may be sensitive. To benefit from its positive effects, spread your consumption throughout the day.

KEEPING CHOCOLATE

Bars

Chocolate reacts badly to temperature variations, such as heat, extreme cold, light, or damp. With this in mind, look for the ideal room in your house. Kept under good conditions, chocolate is very stable and will keep for many months. Once opened, wrap well in kitchen foil and store in a tightly sealed container.

Powders

Bitter cocoa powder is very susceptible to variations in humidity and will soak up ambient moisture, clumping together or forming lumps. Keep it in a hermetically sealed box and store well away from any sources of damp, such as the cooker or sink.

Mousses

Mousses are rich in fatty matter and will absorb and take on the flavors and aromas around them. When made, cover them closely so that they have no contact with the exterior.

Home-made truffles and bouchées

Truffles are like mousses, so take the same precautions. They are also very susceptible to damp. If you want to store them in the refrigerator, where there can be a lot of moisture, protect them with double or triple wrapping.

Cakes

To keep well they should never be left to cool in the pan they have been cooked in after the initial minute or two. When cool they should be wrapped in kitchen foil and then in plastic wrap.

Creams

Store in the refrigerator, covered to prevent the cream drying out or absorbing smells from other foods nearby.

CACAO VARIETIES AND CACAO GRANDS CRUS

Despite similarities, remember that there are many kinds of chocolate. There is a world of difference between a simple bar that is perfectly good but lacking in character and a mouthful of a great Ivory Coast premium chocolate.

Cacao varieties

Criollos

Criollos come from cacao trees that are very susceptible to disease, the terrain, and parasites. They are low yielding and need a lot of care. The beans vary in shape and color but they make very aromatic chocolates that are almost flower-scented and only slightly bitter.

Forasteros

There are several subspecies of forastero—amelonada, para, or maranho, for example—all of which are hardy and productive. Worldwide, these are the most widely cultivated cacao trees, with a relatively neutral flavor profile, although this varies depending on the areas of production and the manufacturing process.

Trinitarios

These are a natural hybrid of the two preceding varieties with, in principle, the advantages of both. They produce subtle, complex, and pleasantly bitter chocolates.

Nacionals

Nacional cacao trees are becoming increasingly rare. They produce very fine cacaos, called "arriba."

Cacao grands crus

These vintage cacaos are found throughout the whole production zone. The great chocolate brands have encouraged this quality initiative, which introduces original chocolates with typical flavors of the local territory, like a great wine or an Armagnac.

East Africa
Madagascar

These grands crus are still quite rare, but certain chocolatiers market them in bars or lozenges containing 75% cocoa. Very aromatic, they are characterized by their balanced flavor and elegant bouquet.

Useful tips
A chocolate without special mention is a blend or mixture created wholly or partly from different varieties. A single origin chocolate is made from cacao of only one variety, either criollo, forastero, trinitario, or nacional.

Western Africa

The great African crus are pure delight. Discover the superb Ivory Coast chocolates, with their hazelnut notes, the rare aromatic varieties from São Tomé, or Ghana's rich and subtle chocolate. Others come from Nigeria, Cameroon, Fernando Pó (Bioko), and the generously mouth-filling chocolate from the Congo.

❦

Central America

The principal grands crus come from Mexico and Costa Rica. They are straightforward, not always powerful, but refined elegant chocolates.

❦

South America

This includes the grands crus of Venezuela (extremely powerful and aromatic dark chocolates), Colombia, Ecuador, Brazil (fairly bitter but fruity chocolate), or the Caribbean islands. Special mention for the superb Jamaican grands crus and those once hailing from Haiti, Grenada, and La Trinité (Martinique).

❦

Asia

Discover the rare crus from Sri Lanka and above all the complex, sometimes sharp but always aromatic ones from Java.

❦

Pacific Ocean

Don't overlook the crus from the Samoan Islands.

Some grands crus
and their zones of origin

Grands crus	Country of origin
Palmira, ocumare, conception	Venezuela
Araguani, alpaco	Ecuador
Guanaja	Honduras
Uba Budo, villa gracinda	Sao Tomé
Manjari, manguro, ampamakia	Madagascar
Los ancones	Dominican Republic
Maralumi	Papua New Guinea

Useful tips

Brazil and the Ivory Coast are the largest producers of cacao beans.
The finest cacaos are said to come from Central and South America.

Over 600 molecules that contribute toward the flavor of chocolate have been identified, some giving almost identifiable notes. Here are a few.
Base aromas: toasted and buttered notes · pyrazynes, aldehydes, etc.
Secondary aromas: fruity notes · esters, etc.
Secondary aromas: hazelnut notes · complex polypeptidics, etc.
Primary flavors: acid notes · organic acids
Primary flavors: bitter notes · dicetopiperazines, etc.
Physical sensations: astringency · phenoloic compounds, etc.

HOW CHOCOLATE IS MADE

Chocolate is the result of a long, slow process where traditional know-how and scientific expertise work together in a unique way. Here is everything you need to know about the principal stages in the making of chocolate.

Fermentation of the beans

Immediately after harvesting, the damp beans and their surrounding pulp are removed from the beans and left to ferment. This crucial operation creates the "taste precursors," the molecules that give the beans their particular taste. Fermentation takes place wherever the beans have been harvested.

Drying the beans

Following fermentation, the beans are spread out on racks to dry. This is when they acquire their typical dark brown color. Next they are piled into jute sacks before being exported around the world to be transformed.

Roasting the beans

In a chocolate manufacturing plant the beans are roasted in large ovens. The "taste precursors" generated during fermentation will develop at this stage. Insufficient roasting makes the resulting chocolate insipid; if roasted too long, the chocolate will be bitter. This is one of the key stages in the manufacture of good chocolate.

Blending the beans

When cool, beans of different origins and varieties are blended to obtain chocolates that contain an even balance of strength and flavor. This process is a bit like making wine by blending a variety of grapes to obtain the best quality.

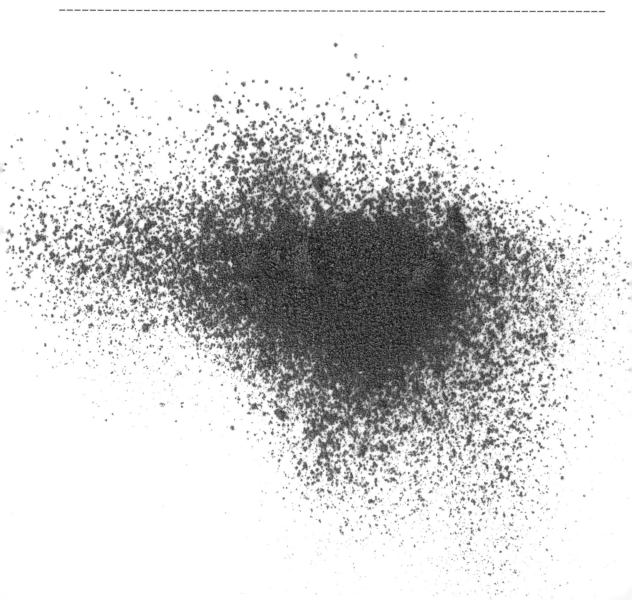

Grinding/refining

The beans are finely ground to make a thick paste called "chocolate liquor," the base ingredient in chocolate, composed of cacao and cocoa butter. The fine grains of cacao are no more than 20 microns long, making it impossible for the palate to perceive them.

Adding ingredients

Chocolate is a recipe: sugar is added, as are an emulsifier and flavorings, depending on the situation. Cocoa powder or cocoa butter may have also been added, according to the brand and the percentages of cacao listed on the wrapper.

Conching

"Conches" are cast iron bowls in which metal beads rotate constantly, grinding the chocolate liquor to stretch it, making it smooth and creamy. The time given to this process is one of the chief factors in the delicacy of the chocolate.

Tempering

Tempering is the art of heating the chocolate to a degree that will make sure of perfect and uniform crystallization of the cocoa butter. This stage determines the sheen of the finished product.

Molding

Finally, the chocolate is poured into molds, cooled, and packaged.

Useful tips
Bitter cocoa powder is made by pressing and filtering the cacao paste obtained during the grinding/refining stage.

155

Index of recipes

Table of contents

CONTENTS
5

☞

CHAPTER 4
MORE ABOUT CHOCOLATE

☞

Index of recipes 156

With thanks to Philippe Da Silva, the chef and friend with whom, over many years now,
I have discovered some of the great mysteries of cookery and patisserie.
Best regards.
Stéphan Lagorce

❧

I should like to thank Isabelle de Margerie for her subtle ceramics and for the
following recipes: chocolate truffles, chocolate spread, dark chocolate fondant,
chocolate and vegetables, chocolate ganaches, chocolate decorations, chocolate mendiants,
and chocolate profiteroles. I should also like to thank Habitat, BHV, Dehillerin, and Mora
for equipment, and G. Detou for specific ingredients.
Delphine Brunet

Graphic Design Dune Lunel aka modzilla!
Translation JMS Books LLP; jackie@moseleystrachan.com
Layout cbdesign